THE KEYS

PROSPE

MANIFESTATION

Love - Faith - Truth - Beauty - Goodness

WALLACE W. FRAZIER

THE KEYS TO

PROSPERITY

MANIFESTATION

Love – Faith – Truth – Beauty – Goodness

Wallace W. Frazier

508 West 26th Street
KEARNEY, NE
68848

402-819-3224 info@medialiteraryexcellence.com

The Keys To Prosperity Manifestation

ISBN (Paperback): 978-1-95808-82-2
ISBN (Ebook): 978-1-958082-80-5

Printed in the United States of America

CONTENTS

The Contents of
This Book Should be
Read With an
Open Mind and a
Receptive Heart

PROLOGUE

Politics has become the religion of many people living on the face of this earth; leaving depleted social, economic and religious belief systems in its wake. Power seekers employ every means at their disposal; confusion, lies and the propagation of division among the masses to perpetuate the grand delusion and illusion of true freedom, also by instigating the notion that they are superior to others and thereby have the right to deprive others of life, liberty and justice.

As we observe affairs around the world, we can see these attributes being played out all over the world but especially in the United States of America, yet we continue to look to some outside entity; a person, a social or religious agency to bring prosperity into our needful and wanting lives. It appears that enough is never enough when the objects sought after are power, money and material things by those who already have wealth or their perception of power, and *we* the people seldom ever 'receive' that which we need.

Over the many centuries that humankind has had a semblance of liberty and justice, a great many people have fallen prey to and have been victimized by the conditioning imposed upon them through religious and social laws and norms that maintain a controlling influence on how and what we believe; leaving many with a sense of hopelessness, fear and despair causing them to believe that they do not have the power to overcome these negative and destructive mindsets.

However, many have awakened to a reality that dispels the lies and they now seek truth. They have come to recognize the hatred of divisive attitudes and behaviors and seek unity through the realization that we are all brothers and sisters, not only among our fellow earthbound humans but also with all celestial personalities, human and superhuman beings throughout the universes of time.

This is the beginning of a new age, dispensation a dispensation in the sense of a period of time given for the ever evolving development of human beings on a world of time and space to manifest a more positive and effective means of obtaining objects of their faith; an age where people begin to acknowledge their inherent powers and abilities and use them to their benefit and provide aid and assistance to those in greater need.

The world is on the brink, on the very precipice of this new dispensation. An age of spiritual enlightenment and faith derived power that will bring to fruition and make manifest their needs and desires. The age in which faith is required to produce the objects, the things that will be needed to survive and even prosper during hard times; the things that will maintain and sustain us through the adventurous and sometimes treacherous and catastrophic events that lie just ahead and beyond.

But ages or dispensation periods do not just abruptly end and another instantly begin. It is a gradual but certain process that inevitably brings a change in the social consciousness, belief systems displayed by the attitudes and behaviors of all people of all nationalities, races and genders on an inhabited world. Perhaps now is the point at which it becomes absolutely necessary for each of us to have an open and objective mind, and realize that there are truths, universe laws and realities that determines how much and to what extent we progress spiritually, mentally, physically, materially and monetarily.

A very wise person has said, "We ask" (for something we need or want) "and the universe responds with opportunities." It is up to us to choose what opportunity to pursue and with the faith we have, explore these opportunities with our actions regardless of our stations in life. Our station in life takes into consideration our social, economic and religious experiences and the opportunities afforded are actions that we can accomplish in our current status.

Perhaps now is the point at which it becomes absolutely necessary for each of us to have an open and objective mind, and realize that there are truths, universe laws and realities that determines how much and to what extent we progress spiritually, mentally, physically, materially and monetarily.

A very wise person has said, "We ask" (for something we need or want) "and the universe responds with opportunities." It is up to us to choose what opportunity to pursue and with the faith we have, explore these opportunities with our actions regardless of our stations in life. Our station in life takes into consideration our social, economic and religious experiences and the opportunities afforded are actions that we can accomplish in our current status.

This is a spiritual undertaking that cannot be exploited or used until we have come to a place and time when we stop putting faith and trust in government and other social and religious organizations for our well-being, and start putting faith and trust in the Ones who can, who will and indeed, who *does* provide all that is needed for our wellbeing and prosperity even in hard times. At All times we should be seeking truth in general and truth in spiritual reality specifically; that is, we should be exerting physical and mental efforts in the pursuit of truth, the recognition and acknowledgment of beauty, and seeking to do good.

At some point something within will feel the urgent need to *know* beyond the things we have been told and otherwise *conditioned* to believe. Our soul, our personality perceives and realizes that there is something more than just the meager physical existence and the seeming never-ending pursuit of unfulfilled dreams, hopes and desires.

There is within the personality code of most of us and our fellow human beings an inherent instinct to acquire material things as a means to secure happiness and joy, but then we realize that any happiness from material possessions are short lived.

For those of our fellows who are in search of truth and the process the actions required that when *applied by faith* brings to fruition and makes manifest the object(s) to which our faith is directed then the information herein may be of great benefit to the *seeker*.

But questions arise. How does one breach the barriers imposed by the pursuit of material wants and basic needs to teach spiritual principles that when applied will surely bring to fruition and make manifest the objects of our desires, and much more? How does one impart a truth that is proven to be more than capable *when applied* of supplying the seekers' every need and much of their desires? How does one encourage and inspire those seekers who are sincere in their efforts to live a genuine Spirit led life of righteousness; adhering to true religion that *will* elicit a much more fulfilling life when they pursue *GOD's* purpose and Will for their life?

How does one convince people to slow down and live simple lives and thereby become disillusioned by the so called 'American dream;' a dream of materialism that has become a nightmare to so many who are willing to do anything in their attempts to obtain such an illusion? How does one compete with the world's version of prosperity which so few have acquired, yet so many relentlessly pursue?

How does one overcome the religious dogma **'about'** Christ Jesus that now prevails in churches and other religious institutions, and rather seek to know and live the religion **'of'** the Christ? How does one shred the veil that perpetuates old *traditions* and rituals that have proven to be fruitless, powerless and unproductive in bringing peace, justice and prosperity to a world of our fellow brothers and sisters so desperately in need of this spiritual, physical and material wellbeing? How does one persuade them to truly seek the Kingdom of GOD, so that when we enter, therein, all these things will be added unto us? What will persuade our fellows to open their heart to the Heavenly Father, and allow Him to reveal as much of Himself as is His Will to so reveal to them?

What is the key to allowing GOD the Father to perform His work in our life, and transform us into the being that *He* wants us to be? How does one persuade others that His way is best? That His way makes us confident in the *knowledge by faith* that we *are* a son or daughter of GOD the Universal Father?

That is the province of GOD the Father. And He is already in the process of solving these questions. Indeed, in eternity they are already solved; for with GOD it is always now. The event of people coming to distrust government and social institutions, and question previously held religious belief system is the beginning of wisdom. Many are becoming aware that greed and corruption are so rampant that seeking the truth and reality that their well being must come from within themselves. People are beginning to turn to the true Source for their wellbeing and prosperity in every aspect of their lives.

Indeed, GOD the Father and all of the angels and beings who perform His Will, continues to "Make people lie down in green pastures," to "renew their soul," (but more on this later). Millions of our fellows have become jobless through no fault of their own. And we are subject to ever increasing natural and man made disasters and pandemics. And the conflicts, wars and civil unrest continue seemingly unabated.

But these are only a few of the methods by which mankind is being taught to slow our roll; to reflect upon our lives, to take stock of life by allowing the 'Spirit Fragment' of GOD our Father in Paradise (our indwelling Thought Adjuster), to lead us to the place where wellbeing originates; from the Great First Source and Center in which all things have their being...*GOD the Universal Father.*

Now more than ever, we need to learn how to apply faith for *practical use*, understanding that faith is more than just a superficial belief in the Lord GOD our Father, and rather, discern that there's more to life, and begin living by applied faith. Living with love for Him, loving Him with all of our heart, our mind, and our strength, and by acknowledging and accepting the truth that He is an unconditionally loving Father; acknowledging and accepting the spiritual reality that we are our Father's children by faith; and as such we should endeavor to have love for our fellows. This is genuine faith!

Faith is to be employed as a *tool* that brings to manifestation the things that we need to live and survive in this life, and to survive through eternity.

Accept and receive son-ship and daughter ship as children of GOD, and realize what that distinction, what that privilege truly means. As faith sons and daughters of our Father we are to be the evidence of His Love by yielding our will to His perfect will, and by bringing to fruition and manifesting the Fruit of the Spirit in our daily lives.

The pursuit of material prosperity becomes secondary manifestations of the objects of our faith. The primary desire to be God-like becomes our most fervent endeavor, not by displaying some false piety which traditional religious thought engenders, but through the knowledge that we are our Paradise Father's children, and as such, we inevitably and invariably come to display the light of love in our many interactive experiences. This then becomes proof that our directed and applied faith has been made manifest...it has come to fruition. Potential reality has become actual reality in our personalities. That which was potential reality has by faith become actual spiritual experiences of value in the life of the individual.

It is often very difficult to relate one's experiences to the experiences of another person; the experiences that have dramatically affected their personal life; things that have made a profound impact on their belief system, bursting their little bubble of previously held social and religious notions.

Realizations of truth comes through discernment and confirmation, by personal revelations to us that what our heart and our mind have been proposing to us as truth is indeed the truth of the matter. And ever so slowly our behavior changes; it must! Because we have a change of mind to the extent that we gradually begin to spiritually perceive, accept and believe as we never thought possible. We are literally *"born again;"* and we begin to *naturally* portray the fruit of the Spirit.

We so often seek revelations that will assist us in this, our mortal life, and they come but we miss them. We miss them because we have been conditioned to expect revelations to come in some dramatic or supernatural way, by some miracle; and in reality, they do, just not in the manner that we may expect.

Our Heavenly Father endowed us with five senses that serve to provide information to our brain which functions as a sensory detector, which our mind processes. The mind of human beings is the dwelling place of the Spirit of GOD that He has apportioned to us... *our spirit.* The Spirit of GOD within us, knows us, all that there is *to* know about us, and He provides directions, guidance and revelations of GOD's Will for each life. Also imparting revelations of truth and enlightenment about spiritual reality; revelations that benefit our life physically, mentally and materially, and opens a whole new paradigm for spiritual growth.

That Spirit of GOD that dwells within our mind has the capacity to assimilate all of the information being received by our brain; allowing us to discern by the *Spirit of Truth* the knowledge imparted to us by the *Holy Spirit* from the *Cosmic Mind,* to help us make the best decisions (choices) in discerning truth, seeing the beauty in all life and giving us the desire to do good in the environment in which we interact with other people and live our life.

And our celestial helpers use it all as a means of helping us make choices that bring us ever closer to the Father, revealing His Will for our life. In this manner He employs every opportunity to facilitate communion with Himself through our faith in His Creator Son Michael, the One who was bestowed on this earth as Christ Jesus of Nazareth.

These are experiences of faith, that when *applied* unquestionably manifests the objects sought. It is a testimony of enlightened experiences; that how through reflection, going back over periods in one's life, the Spirit of GOD brings to our awareness the obvious working of the Heavenly Father for our good as we, by faith, proceed to do what we believe to be His Will. We may not have thought that what we were enduring was for our good at the time, and it certainly didn't seem positive that what we were doing or about to do was in accordance with the Heavenly Father's Will, nevertheless, we proceed by faith, and faith proves itself.

But then, like a veil being lifted from over our eyes, it became obvious; the process He used, His method of working in our individual life, through our previous experiences to bring to fruition His Will and purpose for our life. This should be a testimony as to how, "seeking *first* the kingdom of GOD," does in truth bring to fruition and makes manifest "all these things;" things we need and the things that are in accord with His Will to make manifest for us.

Many revelations will open to you when you start this journey; revelations continually and thoroughly disillusioning you from belief systems and things like fruitless religious notions and pursuits; stuff that you may have once considered important and true, that once enlightened by the Spirit of Truth, shook you to the very foundation of your soul.

Other factors which make it difficult for someone to relate to another's personal experiences is that, every person perceives their own reality based on their specific backgrounds; their own experiences in the environments from which they came, and the influences of and interactions with other people.

Environments change every day, every minute. We encounter people and things that continually expose us to ever changing circumstances and situations and prompt some kind of response from us, either positive or negative.

These are but a few factors that bare on a person's own personal, social, and spiritual and or religious beliefs; and each influences their perception of everything else, and no two people's beliefs, environment and experience are ever exactly the same.

Nevertheless, it is the intent and purpose of these narratives to at least spark some provocative thought processes that may bring to your reality a different perspective; a perspective that is both enlightening and inspiring, and which may be the very thing you've been seeking. You have been seeking, haven't you?

It is not the intent of this author to portray some personal attribute of super intellect or of having a holier-than-thou behavior and mentality. There are far too many of those attitudes already. It truly is not meant to come across that way. Besides, those kinds of attitudes and behaviors are a turn-off and would undoubtedly be such to those who read these narratives as well.

We should be under no delusion as to who we are as sons and daughters of GOD*!!!* Do you not believe that, "to as many as received Him" Christ Jesus "to them He gave power to become sons of GOD?" And if you do not claim, receive and profess your son-ship or daughter-ship of GOD, then *you* are missing the mark! And you don't *know* what you're missing!

There will be some who will consider the contents herein as heretical at best, or as being deceptive at worst. Again, that is not the case. But you have the capacity and ability to decide for yourself. For some of the Pharisees and others of Jesus' day considered Him to even be of the devil, casting out demons by the devil or Beelzebub.

And when thoughts generating in some people's mind, thinking, that you seek to compare yourself to Jesus and they express such thoughts verbally, well you should respond with a resounding and an unequivocal...*yes I am!* Who else is qualified? Who else is most worthy for any and all of us to compare ourselves to, and try to emulate in spirit, if not indeed? If you are not comparing yourself to Christ Jesus, the Deliverer, the Savior, then again you've missed the mark... by a long shot.

Lucifer whom most people think of as Satan and the devil-left his *mark* on this world during the last rebellion in this universe against GOD and Christ Michael. Then there was the defection of Adam and Eve by their submission to Lucifer and the Planetary Prince of this world at the time, and their subsequent expulsion from the Garden of Eden. All of these events seriously affected the normal spiritual developmental plan for humankind on *this* world.

Some of you are probably wondering, "What is he talking about... Christ Michael?" Truth seekers would want to know! The truth *will* amaze you!

Be overjoyed that the Creator Son decided to personally bestow Himself in this world by being incarnated as Christ Jesus of Nazareth. Our survival and eventual ascension to Paradise depended on it; and not just our survival, but also the survival of inhabitants on other worlds in Christ Michael's universe as well.

It is the desire, the hope that those who read the material within these narratives will grasp the humble and sincere attempt to portray the knowledge, the revelation of truth as he has experienced it in his life.

Even now these truths continue to perpetuate hope and motivation to love *all* human beings as they truly are...our brothers and sisters. It is often a difficult task, no doubt! But at times we may not particularly care for the attitudes and behaviors, or enjoy the company of even one of our blood siblings. That is something 'we all' must strive to improve upon if our world and its inhabitants are to overcome these non-progressive attitudes and behaviors.

The love that is hoped to be elicited from these narratives and these words are initiated by the truth of discovering who we truly are as sons and daughters of GOD our Father, and *that* truly gives meaning and purpose for seeing and loving each person as our brothers and sisters.

It is a love with inherent power that provides guidance as to the manner in which we apply the measure of faith we have been given, to make manifest the things that the Father has to give us; relying on those learned truths and processes that we have discovered along our journey.

Truth is the power eliciting element that releases the liberty of real freedom, and it provides the assurance and trust that in due time the *object* of our applied faith will manifest itself in our reality. Then we begin to in joy, enjoy all the benefits that come because of the Father's Love for us, His children, and because of our ever increasing and improving love for Him and our fellow human beings.

If we are dedicated seekers of truth, in our search, along our journey, perhaps your personal experiences may cause you to view your life experiences in a new light. Without a doubt, in your *search* for truth you will be graced and blessed by an enhancement to your life that will benefit you and others whom you encounter and who encounter you. And by faith in our Heavenly Father, and His Creator Son of our universe, may we soon come to live a life of spiritual, material, and physical prosperity and well-being; as it comes to fruition by the ways and means of the Spirit of GOD within each of us.

PERCEPTIONS OF GOD THE FATHER AND HIS KINGDOM

From the times before Christ Jesus walked among the people of this world there has been many perceptions and concepts about who GOD is. Since the beginning of the institutional religions, those in leadership positions have sought to condition the minds of mankind to conform to their belief system, and they have been very successful.

These so-called religious leaders are still effective in imposing fruitless belief systems into the minds of many young people and seniors in particular. The parishioner absolutely believes what the religious leader believes, placing *them* on a higher religious pedestal than they think that they are. These believers have become hardened in their conditioned beliefs, even to the extent of totally discounting truth when it's right before their eyes.

Yet who can blame them when they have been bombarded with doctrines of fear and guilt? And perhaps not so ironically, these are the two most destructive attitudes or attributes that disallows spiritual growth and creativity by faith, for faith is incompatible with doubt, fear and guilt. Fear prevents one from stepping outside of their comfort zone, stagnating their spiritual growth and progress and keeps them from being able to envision or imagine anything other than what they have been told. Even when something doesn't make any logical or reasonable sense, church members are very reluctant to question their leader. Rather than admonishing and inspiring church members to use their own Spirit indwelled minds and seek truth, instead, religious leaders implant images of a wrathful, vengeful and sometimes hateful GOD into their minds as a means to keep them in line.

Once my eldest grandson and I were discussing this concept of GOD and the devil and Satan, and he made an interesting observation. He said, "Granddad, if we listened to these preachers, poor human beings don't stand a chance!" I asked him what he meant, and he explained, "On one hand you've got a vengeful GOD whose scrutinizing everything we do so as to punish us for doing something wrong, and just waiting for the chance to condemn us to hell; and on the hand you've got the devil putting all kinds of temptations and burdens in our way to make us do wrong. We're in a no win situation". "How interesting" I thought. "Here is this young man who has much more insight into spiritual reality than those of my generation and older."

When devoting some thought on the matter as to why my grandson could be so insightful and wise if you will, I concluded that he is of a generation, the millennials and the so called, gen-z's, who have not been so thoroughly conditioned and indoctrinated by such misconceptions about GOD. He doesn't have to be deprogrammed or disillusioned from such misguided concepts. Therefore, he has no problem being open minded and objective. Almost instinctively they pick up on inconsistencies and just plain errors.

Guilt is another villain that robs us of the ability to *apply* faith. Though having a guilty conscious usually means that one knows that they have done something hurtful or harmful to others, it also means that this is something to remedy by seeking forgiveness from those they have hurt and from the Father..."Forgive us our debts as we also have already forgiven our debtors." If we have asked for forgiveness and guilt still prevails, then it is an indication that we have not forgiven ourselves or we don't believe that we have been forgiven. It's called *doubt* and there can be no effective faith where doubt looms.

To those who are so inclined to contemplate and speculate about heaven and the hosts of beings occupying the spiritual realms; and for those that postulate about who GOD the Father truly is, there are as many perceptions of Him as there are people occupying this earth (Urantia).

Personal ideas abound regarding the Father of Christ Jesus of Nazareth; the Father that He so often spoke of and proclaimed, and who He came to this earth to reveal, giving to mankind the true character and attributes of the Heavenly Father; to declare just what His kingdom consists of and where it is. But who is He, our Father and the Creator of all things?

We cannot speak to who the Heavenly Father is to others, but we can speak to who He is to us as an individual, and how we have come to know Him as He has revealed Himself to us. Nevertheless, we *can* bear witness to the realization of having a truer understanding of the Father, and that these revelations have engendered a very new and different sense of reality for us...an all encompassing spiritual reality.

The spiritual manifestation of these revelations renders a whole new perspective of the Father's love; His compassion and His Will that all of His created beings with intelligence should come to be like Him. It causes to spring forth in our heart the assurance of survival through the ages to come as we venture on our journey and ascend to Paradise. The Heavenly Father's grace and mercy and *our* choosing by faith to survive and reach this blessed estate, provides the reassurance that we will indeed and in truth, dwell in Paradise and *be* like GOD our Father.

The dwelling place of the Spirit of GOD is within us, in Paradise and everywhere else. And the more we yield to the Will of our Father, the more our minds expand and gradually encompasses to the finite extent that we can, the magnitude of all that He *must* be as the *Creator*, being the Paradise Father of His Creator Sons of many universes. We should, in humility, come to realize that He is infinitely much greater than any human mind could ever hope to we should, in humility, come to realize that He is infinitely much greater than any human mind could ever hope to comprehend...ever, throughout time. We come to realize that the only way to truly know the everlasting Father is to some day in eternity, to become as He is and someday fulfill His edict to "Be you perfect even as I am perfect."

This you will come to see through spiritual eyes; for this is a spiritual reality and yet it encompasses even the reality of our present physical existence. It is a reality in which the Paradise Father of the Grand Universe is the Great First Source and Center of all things.

The Paradise Father is known throughout this Universe as the Universal Father, He is GOD the Seven Fold, and in all of His Grand and Master Universes His Will is done and shall be done.

Much adoration, praise, honor and glory is given to Christ Jesus our Lord and Savior, as well it should. All that we can give Him in our love and praise is not enough, yet He is satisfied with even that which we in our sincere human capacity can offer. He truly understands human beings and all beings in His Universe. As our Father Brother He has compassion for the human condition, whatever those conditions may be. Albeit, much of the human condition appears to thrive on confusion and errors. Many people even think that Jesus Himself was and *is* the Father that He was referring to when He spoke of the Father in heaven. How perplexing is that?

Traditional religious doctrine has been very effective in placing GOD in a well defined box of its own making in an effort to define Him who is indefinable, and attempting to explain Him who is unexplainable. Undoubtedly some of the many reasons there are so many denominations and religious belief systems. Most religions and faiths of mankind seeks to make the Father conform to their beliefs of who He is, actually making Him very small in their life. The Father can work in your life, *only to the magnitude that you perceive Him, and only to the extent that you allow His Will to be your will.*

Rather, mankind should allow the Father to reveal Himself to them by the ways and means of the Mystery Monitor, the Spirit of GOD who dwells within the minds of all intelligent human beings... as well as in those who are not so intelligent, but who nonetheless are willing to receive the Spirit of Truth, which in reality is the Spirit of Christ Jesus which was poured out upon all flesh on the day of Pentecost. For only by knowing the Son can you in any way truly perceive the Father.

It is He, the Mystery Monitor, a Spirit Fragment of the Paradise Father through which revelations of the Father and His Will for each person is individually revealed. The Spirit of Truth confirms that the revelations are true...if indeed they are, and confirms that it is not just our own ego attempting to get bolstered.

The Heavenly Father is knowable to each person to the extent that He reveals Himself to them; to each person.

On an individual basis He reveals His character traits and His personality attributes, and through His ministering spirits He seeks to inspire and guide us, His children, to do what is in our inherent ability to attempt and accomplish; to acquire the same creative attributes and traits as those of Himself. And it is to those creative attributes and traits that mankind should aspire to attain.

The Father wants us to know Him but only to the extent that we are ready to receive His revelations; as *He* deems us capable of absorbing and managing, and as we are ready to *receive* them. He gives us as much truth as we can assimilate and process into our life experiences at any given time in our life.

Indeed, the Father wants us to *live* the liberty and freedom that knowing the truth elicits; the revelation of this truth, truly and actually produces the abundant life that Christ Jesus proclaimed that He came to give.

When Christ Michael, the Master Creator Son of GOD decided to make His final bestowal here on earth and be incarnated as a human being, His purpose for coming to this world, earth, was to reveal the true nature, attributes and behavior of His Paradise Father. Our Father as well! He purposed to dispel the misbegotten notions about the Heavenly Father as being a vengeful and wrathful Father; a Father who requires little provocation to rain down His fierce vengeance in anger upon the disobedient people inhabiting this planet.

Even the casual but observant reader of the Scriptures can discern the difference in attitude and behavior of the GOD described in the Old Testament and the loving, kind and Fatherly demeanor of the Father as expressed and proclaimed by Christ Jesus of Nazareth in the New Testament. What? Did He suddenly decide to change His personality or His attitudes and behavior? No, He did not! GOD the Paradise Father never changes. People generally perceive things as they have been and are conditioned to perceive them. Long years of institutionalized and socialized religious teachings have hardened peoples' beliefs and ultimately their perception of the Heavenly Father.

"When once you grasp the idea of GOD as a true and loving Father, the only concept which Jesus ever taught, you must forthwith, in all consistency, utterly abandon all those primitive notions about GOD as an offended monarch, a stern and all powerful ruler whose chief delight is to detect his subjects in wrongdoing and to see that they are adequately punished, unless some being almost equal to himself should volunteer to suffer for them, to die as a substitute and in their stead. The whole idea of ransom and atonement is incompatible with the concept of GOD as it was taught and exemplified by Jesus of Nazareth. The infinite love of GOD is not secondary to anything in His divine nature."

You should understand that people in those times harbored primitive concepts of who GOD the Father truly is; and they perceived GOD in the manner that Moses the great leader, painstakingly and pretty much, permanently embedded in their minds. Yet he had a purpose for persuading those whom *he* led out of Egypt to conform to and comply with the laws *he* established and beliefs that *he* instituted. Moses had the awesome tasks of leading not only the Israelites out of Egypt, but the many other non Jewish people, gentiles that took the opportunity to make a hasty escape from Egypt as well. He had to maintain order and strict control of that large number of people. Many of these Jew and gentiles worshiped idols and other gods of Egypt, or worshiped idols made of wood, stone or metal from some other religious belief, custom or tradition.

He also had the more difficult task of instituting civility and order, using every means to influence and persuade them, most often by imposing hard and harsh penalties upon them for breaking his laws and commandments; He even resorted to tricking them into submission and obeying of the Ten Commandments.

These practices and forms of worship they continued even before coming anywhere near the so called…promised land. And he used every method, tactic and resource at his disposal to develop within their hearts and within their minds, the concept of the One GOD, who became known as "YAHWEH."

Between the period intervening between Moses and Christ Jesus, fear was the main method employed by the religious leaders and even some of the prophets, to gain adherence to religious and secular laws of those times.

And When Christ appeared on the scene there were at least five religious sects recruiting converts to their particular forms of beliefs and practices; among whom were those mentioned in Scripture, the Pharisees, Sadducees and Scribes. But there were also the Nazarites of which John the Baptist was a staunch believer and practitioner, and there was also the Essenes.

These sects held true to their beliefs and ritualistic practices to the extent that those not believing their particular doctrines were summarily branded heretic or branded with some other demeaning and guilt evoking label.

Needless to say, the people of Jesus' time on earth had a very confusing time deciding just what the true path was to the GOD they had come to believe in. Much of the same confusion exists still today! Some discovered at the cost of their life, the penalty for teaching and preaching against the customs, doctrines, principles and traditions of the more powerful sects of the time; especially sects like the Pharisees and Sadducees.

And then came Jesus of Nazareth, claiming to be the "Son of Man" which many didn't even know what that meant. "Son of Man?" They probably thought, "of course he's the son of man;" thinking in terms of Him being the son of Joseph the carpenter.

Few of them ever realized that He chose to refer to Himself as "the Son of Man" after being inspired by material He read about Enoch the prophet who often used the term, and it seemed appropriate and applicable to Him.

But this "Son of Man" came proclaiming GOD as His Father; His Father in heaven who sent Him to reveal the Father to humankind, and He came talking about the Kingdom of GOD. He came teaching liberty from the bondage caused by imposed religious and social laws requiring adherence to the customs and traditions of men which holds people in guilt ridden captivity, for no one was able to comply with so many religious laws and traditions. Even those who imposed them did not adhere to them. And He came proclaiming freedom from the shame and the myths and superstitions that enslave people with mentally delimiting, spiritually debilitating and faith nullifying doubt, fear and guilt.

But He also professed to be the Son of GOD and that was more than they could tolerate. And it was those so called "godly" and religious men that caused the crucifixion of Christ Jesus.

Hmmm, wonder how many people who are devoted churchgoers and practitioners of their weekly rituals and traditions, who revel in their own self-righteousness like the Pharisees and Sadducees did would crucify Christ Jesus if He had chosen to live today rather than at the time that He did? How many so called *Christians* would not even recognize the truth that His teachings embrace, or recognize the beauty and goodness of the Kingdom of GOD that Christ Jesus so readily proclaimed as being accessible to all people of the earth and to beings all throughout His Universe; accessible without adhering to man's-imposed burdens? Who would be one of those yelling, "Crucify Him! Crucify Him! Crucify Him? Some people dogmatically and vehemently refuse to come out of the comfort zone that they have become so accustomed to; and they stubbornly resist the exciting and knowledge filled adventure that awaits them to experience the freedom and liberty that comes from knowing the truth.

There is way too much emphasis placed on the horrible death of Jesus, caused by the very beings that He created. Instead, emphasis should be given to His teachings and the life that He lived while on earth. Traditional believers think that His death was some sort of sacrifice for the sins and iniquities of humankind; that He came to atone for the sins of all humanity, the sins which came as the result of Adam and Eve's supposed eating of the forbidden fruit in the Garden of Eden.

While the story of Adam and Eve as written in Scripture- may perhaps make a nice bedtime story for children, the truth is that Christ Michael came for the express purpose of revealing the Father to humankind. He as much say's so! And He came to inspire mankind to seek to be like GOD the Father by inviting them into His kingdom, the kingdom of GOD; admonishing people to acknowledge and accept the truth that He is our Paradise Father and we are His sons and daughters.

As best He could, Jesus the Christ strove to show the *potential* that every human being has to apply and *employ* faith as a son and daughter of GOD, to make manifest and bring to *actuality* the objects of our faith; albeit, He had the difficult task of demonstrating this to primitive thinking people, choosing only to use His supernatural abilities and power in accordance with the Father's Will.

Although the people of today have *evolved* tremendously materially, socially, technologically and otherwise, many still hold to unrealistic and untrue beliefs about the Paradise Father and His Kingdom; especially beliefs about the many beings that make up the Heavenly hosts, and even beliefs about heaven and our journey there; beliefs that ever prohibits true spiritual growth through understanding, knowledge and wisdom, and keeping spiritual growth to the level of mere Christian held principles and doctrines. Christianity has served its purpose. The principles and doctrines of Christianity has done much to inspire humanity to accept our fellows, other people as our brothers and sisters teaching the precepts of the "Golden Rule." But much conflict and animosity to Christian believers and the Christian Faith in general has emerged from the seeming inability of professed Christians to actually and literally practice the Golden Rule.

They can't seem to get the part that says to, "do unto others as you would have them do unto you" quite right.

Nor have they come close to loving their enemies or even loving their neighbor as they love themselves. Christianity has done much through the evangelistic efforts of those inspired to teach the masses of people about Christ Jesus. But they can only teach and preach to the extent of their knowledge, which, in the grand scheme of things is limited to their own religious experiences. There is much more truth to be known; truth that they know not of; and truth that will not be found in institutions of religious learning, nor even in Biblical scripture.

Fellow brothers and sisters, there is a much larger concept and perception of the Father and His Kingdom. Both the spiritual realm of existence and this physical, this material realm of existence is only a mere particle of His kingdom.

If you can imagine a being who has powers and abilities that exceeds those of Superman about one trillion times, then you would be at the entrance to the ballpark, at best you might be *in* the ballpark.

The more we can acknowledge and accept GOD the Father as *our* Heavenly Father, and the more we realize that His power and abilities are infinitely greater than anyone's mind capacity can even begin to imagine, then the more GOD conscious we become, and the greater will be *our* capacity to exercise the faith that has been apportioned to us. You will in earnest truly begin to experience spiritual assurance and confidence that the Father loves you absolutely and unconditionally, and that His Will for you is only that which is for your good.

The Heavenly Father and the Eternal Son is personified in Christ Michael, who was made incarnate in Christ Jesus of Nazareth. Those who knew Him then, His life and teachings, and those today that study and envision His life and to whom His Word is revealed, should by reading the Scriptures perceive the confidence and trust that Christ relied on in the Father. He seeks always to do the Will of the Heavenly Father, as we all should. And in everything we should give Him thanks, having the faith and trust that whatsoever we do *is* the Will of the Father concerning us.

The kingdom of the First Source and Center, GOD the Father, is infinite and everlasting as He the Father is infinite and everlasting. The Father is Perfect, He is Love, and in His Perfect Love He demonstrates perfect order, organization and harmony.

His children display these same attributes in their attempts to be perfect, in their attempts to be godly, like GOD. But do people really think that once they depart this earth, that they are going to suddenly become so perfect through the death of Christ Jesus and the experience of their own death, that they will be instantly ushered into the presence of GOD Almighty? Wow...that's pretty arrogant!

"As Above, so below! A small phrase that has immense meanings. We must look at, just what is below?   Okay...there are governments and these governments have laws, protocols and hierarchies.

There are countries that have defined borders with citizens natives born in those countries but they also have migrants that come from other countries whether they are just passing thru or taking up residence in them, and these countries have states and cities within them.

Now...What is above? If you will, envision spiritual realities of hierarchical governments and beings that far transcends those that are below; a hierarchy where earth (Urantia) is just the initial preparation ground of our ascending progression. Then we transition, through death to our next world in the System, waking up in the resurrection halls of the mansion world(s). Next, we transition by another ascension method other than death to the Constellation worlds, then to Universe worlds for more spirit training; then to the Minor Sector, the Major Sector, then to the Super universe worlds where we will be close to being true spirits. After which we ascend to Havona in the Master Universe for spirit perfection, then finally to Paradise where we will stand before the Father as perfected beings in eternity.

As it is with everything, there is a process. And in our progression to be like GOD, there is an ascension method that every being that chooses to survive *must* follow. Can you not see that the process began at your birth and you have progressed in this life to the place where you are right now? Perhaps you haven't progressed materially, but you surely have mentally and maybe spiritually whether you consciously realize it or not.

You know more now than when you were born. The progressive evolution of mind, body and soul through your life's experiences, and irrespective of any secular education you may attain along the way. Progressive experiences have spirit value. Spirit values being those experiences that we carry with us through our ascension to Paradise and beyond.

Not only have we progressed, everyone and everything in life at this point in time has also progressed; you can call it evolution, cause that's truly what it is.

Change is inevitable. Everything, everywhere changes from one state of *being* or state of *existence* to another. Nevertheless, the thing changing may retain a semblance of that which it was originally; and these changes happen gradually over time. You were once younger than you are now, but you have become older one millisecond at a time. And that list of changes which we have personally experienced goes on and on throughout eternity; you are still you but you've *changed* from one state of being to another. And your progression continues on *long* after your transition from this earth thru death...if you choose to survive.

GOD the Father does not change. He *was*, *is*, and He will always be the same, always...Perfect! His steadfastness is why we can rest assured that what He promised He will deliver as we are ready to receive it. He promised us eternal life and He has long ago provided the means, the protocol and the method by which we obtain it, but we must prove ourselves as sons and daughters of the Father by exercising our faith each and every step along this journey to perfection.

There is much to learn along this journey; much truth which is of spiritual value that will be of great worth as spiritual realities are revealed to us, if we will but allow the Spirit of Truth, the Spirit of Christ Jesus to discern and separate that which is truth about our Father and His kingdom and our perceptions in this reality from that which is fiction.

You will come to understand that the kingdom of GOD the Father is a literal kingdom. It exists in Paradise as His eternal abode and it exists outside of Paradise, in the many universes of time and space which is also His kingdom. But His kingdom is also in the hearts and minds of all those who acknowledge and accept Him as their Father, and who accept Christ Jesus as their Creator and as their Lord and Savior; He who made our eternal survival possible.

POTENTIAL MADE ACTUAL BY FAITH

The fact, the truth that the potential for anything and everything to become a reality should be of enormous reassurance that what we ask of the Father is within His purview to accomplish. With such potential we should be thrilled and confident, and trust that what He has is ours for the asking and receiving by faith. It should produce hope that enhances our faith capacity to levels that most of our fellow brothers and sisters have not yet experienced.

Think of it! There is nothing that has ever before existed, or that exists right now, or that will ever exist that was not *potential* first. Potential supplies the substance for the *hopes* that everyone uses, albeit this potential is preexistent, we all still employ hope as an element of our faith.

Potential is the static condition that *anything possible* is in before it becomes active; before it becomes actual and real, before it becomes something that can be experienced. The dictionary defines *potential* as: "Possible, but as yet not actual; having a latent possibility or likelihood of occurring, or of doing or becoming something."

Potential is pre existent before we perceive it; before the potential for something even exists in our mind. In a sense, it exists before it exists (that can be mind blowing!) . But it becomes a little easier to understand when it is realized that the Universal Father is the 'Great *First Source and Center*' of all things. The *pattern* for all of creation, everywhere, for all times and for every space originates in Him from the Isle of Paradise, the Universal Father's eternal abode. And the Isle of Paradise exists in eternity where there is no time.

Time has relevance to our Father because it is relevant to His creations' progression to perfection...over time. As for potentiality and actuality, in eternity there is no difference; *actuality* happens simultaneously with *potential*; the beginning of a thing is the end of a thing, and the end of a thing is the beginning. As it is thought, it is instantly done. Yet it takes time outside of eternity for it, whatever the potential becoming actual is, to materialize in time and space. There is only difference and distinction, consequent in time and space.

Only time and space prevails before the potential substance the preexistent form of the hoped for thing becomes actual, when it becomes manifest into reality as evidence of your faith.

Where potential exists, that is, after the potential for something is perceived by or conceived in our mind, *conditions* must be favorable or that conditions are certain to become favorable at some point *in time*, that hence, by faith you perceive it to be the Will of the Father that the now *existent potential object* that you hope for comes to fruition, that it *will* indeed become actual.

So, what are these conditions and how do they come together to make the object that is potentially existent become actual? They are too numerous to name. And we would not have the capacity or the ability to find the correct combinations of ingredients to stimulate whatever forces are required to make the potentially existent object manifest into reality. Our faith is what accomplishes that. For it is our faith that motivates our Father to mobilize the beings of the Heavenly hosts to *make* the conditions favorable and right to ensure the manifestation of the existent object, which for the moment only exists in our mind.

Mankind has been given the capacity to realize that the things that they accomplish, the buildings they build and the material things that they produce have originated first from a *source* other than our own mind. The mind is the receptacle that receives revelations, patterns, and processes and develops the means by which to produce things and by which we progress. And once the pattern is realized in the mind, the object is no longer pre-existent potential; it becomes purely existent potential, and awaits activation by the required conditions coming together to give momentum to the forces that makes the "potential" object an "actual" one.

With knowledge and understanding of nature by the Holy Spirit into mental images, and then designs for the house start to emerge from the state of pre-existent potential to existing potential in the mind.

But that's only the beginning of the conditions that must be met before the house is a reality. Further conditions include having enough money to buy or build a house, which most certainly necessitates the condition of having a job or another source of income, and then the acquiring of a mortgage loan, getting a contractor to build the house and so on until the house that was once only in one's mind becomes a reality.

These are conditions that are of a material nature and which have come to be standard conditions that must be met by anyone. There are standard conditions that apply to making manifest many material objects. But in spiritual, physical and even material matters where faith is the method applied to make manifest the potential object of our desires or need, conditions that must be met are not so standard...at least not to mankind, nor or they available for mankind's manipulation.

When faith is used *applied and exercised*, but more so, when it is the Heavenly Father's Will that we receive the object to which our faith is directed the object that has the potential of becoming actual then conditions of a spiritual nature are required. Some conditions are met by the *actions*, the *work* that we are *led* to perform; by the effort we exert and the *energy* we expend toward bringing the potentially existent object to actuality. That is our part in the joint venture to bring the faith object from the spiritual realm to this physical and material realm.

Other conditions are those that only spiritual beings can and do perform behind the scenes; "the evidence of *things unseen*." And over time, whether the *substance* of things hoped for is of a spiritual nature understanding, knowledge, wisdom or Fruit of the Spirit etc, or whether it is a *substance* of a purely material or physical nature that is hoped for, it will by faith in due time and in its due season be made manifest.

Conditions can be and can include many things or a few things. One thing is certain, whether using faith or natural means to make manifest the object that is as yet in a potential state, there *are* conditions that must be met. First, and foremost, there must be belief that a thing can be done; if faith is being applied then believing and trusting in GOD to cause the spiritual conditions to come together that brings the object to actuality is absolutely essential; or if by purely natural means, having belief and trust, faith that we ourselves or someone else can produce the thing is necessary.

Either way we believe that we will receive the object, and that it will be made manifest into reality… actuality.

Secondly, there must be *trust* in our Paradise Father and His Sovereign Son that it is Their Will that we receive the potential object, or if by using purely natural means, then having faith and trusting in yourself to have the capacity and the ability to meet the conditions that makes manifest the desired object.

People will not always possess the ability or the capacity to make manifest the object by natural means regardless of how much effort they exert simply because of their inherent limitations; the limits that their environment and their station in life and that they have put on themselves restricts them, and especially if it is not the Father's Will that we receive the object. Faith does not circumvent or supersede the natural means of bringing the conditions together. It sometimes simply puts in motion the elements that *over time* would have happened naturally and brings to manifestation the object of your faith sooner, *as* you are prepared to receive it. You will receive it simultaneously when the conditions are right and met, and when you are ready, when you are spiritually mature enough and you have the requisite preparation for the potential object to be made manifest.

THE ABUNDANT LIFE

It is truly a difficult prospect for many people in the societies and cultures of today's world to even consider having or living the abundant life. That of course depends on what one considers the abundant life to be.

It is part of the human experience that some acquire wealth, fame or prestige and power, and all these things they may perceive as living the abundant life. Their perception of the abundant life is one of having plenty of whatever they want; a perception that was encouraged by parents and nurtured mostly by the environment into which they were born and raised. The environment of their homes and communities, the interaction of people with whom they associate, the lessons learned in schools, churches and other institutions form their own personal experience. All of these external elements exert tremendous influence on shaping attitudes and behaviors. These things also exert influence on most people. Having material prosperity contributes to the notion that having material where-withal is living the abundant life...and for many it is.

Then there's the flip side of the coin; those who are born in poverty, or close to it, whose daily existence consists of obtaining food and the basic needs for themselves or perhaps for their family by whatever means necessary. They are so preoccupied with survival that seldom does the thought of ever rising above their current level of existence cross their minds. And again, their environment and all the elements and conditions that are attached, preconditions them to not even attempt to pursue anything like the abundant life.

Indeed, to be graced with an extra portion of meat, or to find potable water to drink, or find shelter in which to take refuge to them may *be* the abundant life, if only for the moment. Those opportunities may not happen often and they dare waste any time thinking about a lifestyle that life has to that point denied them, or that they have denied themselves.

These people live in the now; taking advantage of what is available now. Their mortal survival is at stake! Ah...but then there's the rim, the edge of the coin which supports both sides. In every society and many cultures there persists to some degree the people who knowingly and willingly or not, make the wealthy wealthier, and also provide support for those who are impoverished. The latter, providing support for the impoverished is far more altruistic, charitable and more preferred, if by none other *than* the impoverished.

These people, those on the rim in this country are the so called *middle class* or the *working class*. Many have decent or sustainable jobs and homes and most of the appurtenances of what has been termed in America, "the American dream;" and they are content! They realize that with life comes problems, trials, pains and troubles, but they deal with them as best they can, still, for them this may be the abundant life.

And there are other ways in which people may consider themselves as having the abundant life; having good physical and mental health, having an enjoyable intellectual and social life, and even having a good moral and religious life...the two are not particularly synonymous.

Yet with all of the physical, material and religious acquirements and accoutrements, is all this having or living the abundant life? Is the possession and use of these things truly living the abundant life that Christ Jesus proclaimed or is it something else? In His discourse about the Good Shepherd, He began with the thief who comes to kill, steal and destroy, but who is the thief?

In the days that Christ walked among mankind, Lucifer and the devil, and Satan and all of their rebellious and disloyal cohorts were very active in and with human beings. It could truly be said that the devil or demons, fallen angels possessed people.

They had both direct and indirect influence upon people which caused those so possessed or so influenced to exhibit abnormal behaviors; but they also instilled false perceptions and teachings about the Father in many more people, much of which still exists today.

And then as now, people latch onto the remnants of those false teachings with dogmatic loyalty and it *kills* any chance of their seeing the truth that Christ came to reveal. And such dogmas deprives them of having a real and genuine spiritual experience, a personal relationship. Rather they seem to be momentarily content with the warm fuzzy *emotional response* received from the eloquent words of a preacher or other speaker, responses to actions in concert with group behavior. Notwithstanding the real and genuine inner spiritual experience received when a truth is revealed or confirmed that resonates within the soul, or when experiencing a sincere time of intimate praise, thanksgiving and worship and it becomes too overwhelming to contain.

He, the thief, *steals* the liberty that the truth enables, and *destroys* the creative process and the *potential power* that graces a true son and daughter of the Father; that truth which makes the potential power actual power to make manifest by faith that which is the Heavenly Father's Will for us.

When liberty is stolen, taken away from you, you are no more than a slave. And what slave except those who escape their bondage can truly be free to live an abundant life? Nevertheless, *conditioning* is an overwhelming force which is seldom even realized because it happens to you so gradually and subtly *over time*.

The victim, if they are aware, or becomes aware that they are being conditioned could possibly summon the will to resist. Therefore, conditioning must be subtle and inconspicuous to the unwary.

That is the taskmaster of tradition. All taskmasters have their tools to keep the master's slaves in line with his rules and demands, so does the taskmaster of tradition.

And its tools are many of the churches and their doctrines, established to create and maintain a way of believing GOD as they want their loyal members to believe and perceive Him; a way of believing that minimizes Him and elevates the church, the preacher and the denomination to which they belong.

But this is the social church, a social organization and *not* the *true church*. The true church consists of those who sincerely and wholeheartedly believe in, and have received Christ Jesus as the Creator Son of GOD and as their Lord and Savior, and those who in earnest seek the kingdom of GOD; those who seek truth and who in essence seek to discover the religion that Christ Jesus practiced...lived.

The abundant life that Christ Jesus was talking about comes about by living a life full of experiences and growth. Oh no! Not my experiences or anyone else's experiences. Rather by finding the Father in their own experiences. The Father whose Will it is that His children be given absolute freedom and liberty to pursue and experience life according to their own choosing.

This is a freedom and liberty however, that comes with the obligation of moral responsibility to the Father, and to us and our fellow human beings. This is a liberty that liberates you from the bonds of traditions that ritualizes religion and makes it stagnate, nonprogressive, unproductive and fruitless. It is a liberty that releases us from the notion that by being a member of an institutional church or organization is the only way to salvation. That's what many who attend these churches seem to believe.

Somehow, they have come to believe that if a person does not go to church, that they are going straight to hell; they are not going to pass go, they're not going to collect two hundred dollars, they are going straight to hell. Poor fellows! How misled they are! Yes! Blind leaders of the blind and they're both going to fall into the ditch. We should believe what the Spirit of GOD reveals to us as truth and not what constant and consistent conditioning would have us to believe is the truth. They are not always the same.

It is the function of the Ancients of Days to judge. That is their province not yours or mine, and they are more than capable, just, righteous and fair in their deliberations and considerations. They have been performing their work for many billions of years and they have many capable subordinates providing input so that their assessment and final edict is just. They don't need anyone's help. Once they pass judgment on you...well...it's a done deal, you are sentenced to extinction (not hell) or you survive. In the case of extinction there will never be any more you.

To understand that there are other beings and personalities in the Grand Universe and learn their various functions in the marvelous kingdom of GOD, this is just some of the liberating truth that encompasses the abundant life. These truths not only liberate us, but they give us a real sense of belonging to something and to Someone much greater than ourselves, for we are sons and daughters of GOD. Such a belief system invigorates us and gives us a real sense of purpose and motivates us to action. It incites within us the yearning to create and to really *experience LIFE*.

The abundant life is having the faith, the confidence and trust in our Father that He will supply all our needs according to His riches in glory. The abundant life is experiencing the manifestation of the object of our faith and the subsequent joy from the knowledge that our Heavenly Father, in His love for His children, has made *faith* the means of providing for we His son or daughter.

The abundant life is having the capacity to forgive others, but also, to forgive yourself; acknowledging that GOD the Father has already forgiven us, and that we must only believe and receive His forgiveness by faith.

Eventually if not sooner we come to realize that the guilt that we feel when we have tried and failed to live by Bible principles, and all the rules that are imposed on us by institutional religion are weights, yokes that severely restrict and inhibit the full exercising of our personality; the person we are and person we were created to be, but also the person we are becoming.

The abundant life comes with the realization that we are ever progressing toward perfection, and that the life we now live on this world is just the preparatory school before advancing to the next level of our existence, and to the next level of our spiritual educational experience. Just as this life has its adventures to challenge us in our many endeavors, the next life of adventure will be of a kind to advance our soul's spirit value through the knowledge, understanding and wisdom wrought by our own personal experiences there as well.

The abundant life is having the assurance without doubt, fear and guilt that no matter what trials and burdens of life we encounter along our journey, we are our Father's children and He wants only that which is for our good. Through whatever He allows us to encounter, if we accept that it is for *our* good, *our* understanding, *our* knowledge and *our* wisdom, that eventually we will be perfect even as He is Perfect.

THE DIVINE YOU AND THE HUMAN YOU

D uring the time in which Christ Jesus lived among humans, He was in truth and every otherwise...human! For those who dogmatically revere the Bible as the word of GOD, you have been taught that Christ laid aside His Godly powers when He was incarnated on earth and became as a human being; and indeed, He did...all of His great powers!

He came as a babe so that He could experience what humans had to endure during the course of their life, their whole life. And He could only have such an experience by going from the beginning of a human life to the end of that life; and by being born by natural means; the usual and normal process by which human beings are conceived.

His purpose was simple. He wanted to reveal the Heavenly Father His Father and ours to mankind; bringing the *truth* about the Father to human beings; His love, His creativeness, His capacity of giving and forgiving, His true essence. And the way He determined best to do that was by being incarnated *as* a human being on this world of His creating. He sought to inspire mankind to become GOD conscious by being among them and showing them the *way* to the kingdom of GOD which is already within them; for where the Spirit of GOD is, there too is His kingdom. And His Spirit dwells within the heart of all of mankind and everywhere else!

Christ Jesus showed mankind that always choosing to do the Will of the Paradise Father is *not only* the *best* way, but also *'the only'* way to discovering the Kingdom of GOD. He showed them the extent of their *potentials* while being human, and while being a son or a daughter of GOD.

Christ Jesus aspired to know all about the human condition; human issues and how people deal with them. He discovered how difficult life can be for people and He came to understand how susceptible and often, how gullible humans are regarding myths, superstitions and their fears; myths that give rise to unrealistic and untrue perceptions about our loving Heavenly Father; superstitions that foster primitive and unprogressive attitudes and behaviors; fears that preclude the hope of receiving the object of their faith, which the First Source and Center, GOD our Father, wants His children to have and use for their benefit and the benefit of others. It takes a fearless person to go into unknown situations, however thoughtful of possible perils, but who after careful consideration determines that the *potential* reward from the effort is worth the risk.

Fear is a delimiting and debilitating emotion that prevents people from acting. When people are overcome by fear they go into a panic mode. Their brain goes into shutdown and bodily functions ceases to operate properly...except for maybe the legs and feet to flee.

Yet Fear is one of the elements on which many religions of today are based. These things, doubt, fear, guilt, and believing foolish myths and superstitions as truths are spiritually limiting, having little or no spiritual value, content, or *practical applicability* because they simply are not true. And doubt, fear and guilt are weights that bind the mind and produces low self-esteem and little or no self-confidence.

Christ Jesus sought the truth all the while he was in human form, and He knew that He had a Divine purpose. But it was not until He attained full *self-realization*, realization of who He truly was both human and Divine, that He in fact and in truth was the Creator of this universe that He persisted in saying that His "hour had not yet come." At that point and until His death (transition) He fully began doing the Will of His Heavenly Father and the work of His kingdom.

As a human, Christ Jesus was limited by many things just as all human beings are; being limited by nature, the environment where He interacted with other people and their personal attitudes, and by their beliefs and behaviors.

Yet even in the flesh He knew the potential that exists in humans; that when faith is applied in truth and activated by works, and when they have come to full self-realization of who they are as sons and daughters of GOD that even human beings with nominal GOD consciousness and self realization can do phenomenal things.

Faith is a powerful tool in our journey to eternity. The Father requires it of all His children. It only takes as little as the grain of a mustard seed. You start out on your journey with at least that much! It's up to us to acquire more; and we acquire more by applying that which we have.

Self-realization is the prelude to the *divine you*; it first encompasses seeking, acknowledging and accepting the truth, and then applying faith based on the truth that GOD the Father has apportioned to us, and trusting in Him *as* our Father. Seeking to know as much about Him as He allows to reveal to us and *truly desiring to know and do His Will, this is being GOD-conscious.*

Receive, accept and acknowledge the true revelations that come to you by means of His Spirit, that Fragment of Himself who dwells within you. Then by faith, acknowledge, accept and receive son or daughtership as a true child of the Most High GOD with all the spiritual benefits and liberty that is automatically attached to this great honor and privilege.

Understand that just as Christ Jesus/Christ Michael the Master Creator Son of GOD came forth from His Father, we also came forth from Him who is also *our* Father. Christ Michael came forth in His capacity as the LORD and now, the Sovereign Master of His creation, *this* universe and all that exists herein; and we came forth in our capacity as a *human* being, a faith son or daughter of the same Father. As a child of GOD, although constrained by time and space, we have the absolute privilege of liberty to think and act by faith.

It is a choice that we must make, to live by the faith that a child of the Father has the right to exercise. We are children of the Universe of Michael and it is a friendly universe when we seek to do the Father's Will.

Liberty is defined as "The freedom to think or act without being constrained by necessity or force." Liberty inherently comes from knowing the truth! But also, what comes with liberty is the expanded capacity of our ability to experience, perceive, understand and believe. Actually, having so strong a belief that it is perceived as knowledge. Knowing; having the knowledge of who we truly are and knowing that our Heavenly Father wants for us *only* that which is for our good. And that which is in our capacity to receive we shall receive. How free are you?

Where institutionalized social religion leaves off in your spiritual development, continue to seek the truth beyond that point. Ask questions! How else will you know? Be persistent in your search for the kingdom of GOD so that "when once you enter, therein, all these things shall be added unto you." GOD and His righteousness are not separate entities. By always seeking to know Him you automatically seek to know His righteousness. The truth is ever revealing and by abiding in the words of Christ Jesus we know the truth as we are capable and have the ability to receive it. Not as someone else perceives it. Seek to do the Will of the Heavenly Father. Discover the truth for yourself...*Be persistent!!!*

Persistence does pay big dividends, even if only in helping us develop patience. But being persistent does much more. It opens doors that might not otherwise open unto us. Some doors can only be opened after knocking -seeking the way to accomplish, attain, and obtain something. But know this! The door only remains open for a specific period of time, as determined by the Father and in accordance with His Will, and our efforts...our works.

It is often difficult to be persistent, particularly after long periods and it seems that the object of our faith is not forthcoming. Though our faith may waiver on the brink of doubting, don't doubt! Push on with the God given strength that He has already provided for us; with the hope that the substance, the object of our faith will be made manifest and yield the evidence that proves that faith was appropriately applied.

You should not relinquish your liberty or quell your faith due to some misplaced loyalty to a book that is basically the historic events of one group or race of people and their primitive belief systems. You should not be beholding to a building or to a person, thinking that they are the only means to your survival or salvation. Especially if therein and by them truth is distorted or replaced with personal interpretations. Teaching and preaching by those who do not really know the truth nor have had a genuine personal relationship with GOD, they can only speculate and give their opinion based on *conditioned responses* that they have been taught, perpetuating and propagating far outdated doctrines and traditions.   We have been indwelt with the Spirit of the Father in Paradise. They are named Thought Adjusters, the *Mystery Monitor* that lives within our mind. Our Spirit through which He can and does speak to us just as He speaks to them… maybe even more so if we listen! For who knows the real motives of men and those of mankind who are in positions of authority? History indicates that their motives usually do not serve the majority of the people. But we *can* know GOD the Father's Will! And we can know that His motives are all about bringing His children to be perfect just like Him. So how do you know what GOD the Father's Will is for your life?

There are various scriptures that leave no doubt as to what   some of the Father's Will is for us and all of His sons and daughters: "You shall love the Lord your GOD, with all your heart, with all your soul, with all your strength, and love your neighbor *as* yourself; this is His all encompassing Will for all of

His children; for all of us to be as one enormous family, for that is truly what we are. We are to exhibit brotherhood or sisterhood to each other, acknowledging the Universal Father as the Father of all. But people often don't know the Will of the Father until the object of their faith has been made manifest. You have received the object that you prayed and meditated for, sometimes for years maintaining faith that it was the Father's Will.

You have listened to the still small voice inside, gently urging you into specific courses of action, and now the Father makes known His Will by bringing to fruition and making the object manifest.

Conversely, if after a period of time, the object of your faith has not come to fruition and you haven't received it, then it may not be for your good to have the object. If you don't get the continual and persistent urgings by the Spirit of GOD in your mind that makes you restless, irritable and dissatisfied until you invariably stop resisting and do as you are being prompted to do, then what you asked for is most likely not the Will of the Father for you regarding that particular faith object; at least, not in the time frame in which you have asked and want it, and maybe not even in *this* life but in another one. If we survive there are many.

People in the societies of today's world seek instant gratification and will go out of their means and reasonable sense to obtain it. They often disregard the impact that the means they employ to obtain what they want will have on others; and despite the impacts on others, the Paradise Father may 'allow' the actions motivated by their belief in self. He may because of their behavior and selfless intentions accommodate them with the thing(s) they desire. Not to encourage or enable undesirable actions and behavior, but rather, to allow those actions and behaviors to run their full course, to come to the end game; the reaping of the seeds that they have sown. But if it is GOD's Will for you to have the object of your faith, then you *will* have it, in this life or another.

If you *acknowledge Him* in all your ways and pray that in every situation and circumstance *His Will* be done, then you can rest in the assurance that *His Will shall be done!* The Father's Will shall prevail either way; whether you pray that His Will be done, or whether you truly want His Will to be done or not!

By faith, proceed! Do what your common sense in agreement with your heart and your mind is telling you is the right thing to do. The Spirit of GOD will lead you in the right work you must do to bring the object of your faith to manifestation. Again, do that what your mind and your heart tells you to do, especially if you believe it may *be* the Will of the Father. We proceed by faith. Remember and know without doubting that "*all things* work together for good to them that love GOD, to them who are the called according to His purpose."

His purpose for your life *is* your purpose and reason for living, and when you seek to realize His purpose for your life, you concurrently begin to find self realization. Gradually over time you will discover the gift your talent that may have lain dormant that the Father endowed you with since birth, and when you seek to develop it, then it is practically applicable to your life, and it becomes the means by which you are to prosper; spiritually, mentally, physically and materially.

But you must be patient and wait for guidance as to how you must proceed, and for the work that you must do to be revealed. This does not by any means suggests being idle, even if it means studying Biblical scripture or the Urantia Book. For the more you actually apply your faith, the more you too will live your life by faith, and display the abilities and character traits as Christ Jesus did when He came to full and total self realization; when He was in complete communication with His indwelling GOD Fragment His Spirit- the Spirit of GOD.

Christ Jesus always displayed and portrayed an aura about him that expressed and exuded complete confidence and trust in the Father, for He now knew that He was the Creator of a vast universe and everything that exists therein. He always had the unqualified and unquantified assurance that GOD the First Source and Center was His Heavenly Father, and if what He asked was the Father's Will then it would come to fruition.

Yours, mine, all of our bodies are only vehicles. Vehicles composed of biologic, chemical and electrical components. Within this magnificent creation called the human being is resident the ability to adapt to practically every given natural condition that mankind may encounter along their journey. Along with the brain which acts as a central processing and distribution station, receiving and sending phenomenal amounts of information via its sensory inputs, these bodies are capable of functioning on a level compatible to the environment in which it finds itself. But these are necessary for mortal survival.

For spiritual survival, this vehicle contains two *endowments*, valuable gifts that our Father has been so gracious to bestow within human beings. The first endowment is your personality which is produced by our Universal Father and distributed to all intelligent beings on every inhabited world by GOD the Eternal Son, the Second Person of the Trinity.

Your personality is you! It is who your Heavenly Father has destined you to be; given the Spirit led or personal *choices* that you make in the environments in which you find yourself.

The Second endowment is a Fragment of His Spirit, *'your spirit,'* which He saw fit to assign to your physical body and therein He abides within your mind. Among the things that this Spirit Fragment does is to reveal the Father to us; to make Himself known to us and also to gather and retain all of our experiences of spirit value in the repositories of the fourth Person of Himself as GOD the Sevenfold, the Supreme Being.

For He knows how well we are progressing spiritually at every step of our ascension adventure and with the guidance by His many ministering spirits, brings us ever closer to perfection. It's exciting, isn't it?

The bodies that contain these two endowments are of little significance, except to serve as a means by which to experience life. It is merely a vehicle that transports the essence of who we are while in the pursuit of our eternal destiny. It provides the sensory input we need to gain knowledge and understanding through experiencing life, and to hopefully develop within us spiritual values; the spiritual attributes and the character that is required for us to obtain the third endowment which is a purely spiritual one... Eternal Life!

The attaining and obtaining of these attributes, values and character is a *process* that unfolds and that we develop during the course of time. They are things of spiritual value that, where upon finally reaching eternal life, we will be as GOD the Father is...Perfect! For in eternity there is no imperfection! That which is imperfect cannot dwell there. Only that which is the perfection of truth, beauty, and goodness abides there.

Imperfection exists only outside of the '*Isle of Paradise,*' in the realms of space and time. Evil is the byproduct that is generated by the difference between perfection and imperfection and it is necessary in order that we can have and make choices. Everything outside of the Master Universe, Havona and Paradise is subject to the effects of evil...potentially. Evil is only activated, that is, it becomes actual when people knowingly and intentionally choose to do harm to their fellows, when they choose to do something other than what they know to be the Heavenly Father's Will; His Will for them as an individual and His Will for all people in general. Seek to do no harm to your brothers and sisters who are on their own mortal quest for spiritual values.

They may often submit to the animalistic tendencies that are inherent to creatures of nature. Allow them to have their own experiences, as the Father in Heaven allows you your experiences.

When you understand and can empathize with your brothers and sisters' behaviors, though frustrating they may sometimes be, then you will be more on the path to actually and naturally bringing to the surface the divine you.

The truth that evil is potentially existent should not be misconstrued to mean that everything in all of GOD's creation and everything in nature is evil. Because it absolutely is not! But it *does* mean that there is the *potential* for evil behavior; behavior that is not conducive to that exhibited by someone seeking to be GOD like, and to someone seeking to do the Father's Will, and to someone seeking to be perfect.

Our Heavenly Father is Perfect, and in His Perfection, He creates, and then He maintains and sustains His creations; the worlds and the many beings that He creates to inhabit these spheres. He does it by employing the beings that He creates to function in their specific roles; and He makes as part of all of His created beings' endowments the ability of creativity and all that each persons' creative package entails.

Do people not already create as an inherent attribute of the human spirit...the Spirit of GOD that dwell in our mind? This is a gift given to us by our Paradise Father. Even without coming to total self-realization or coming anywhere near it, our limited creativity should speak to how creative, productive and progressive the human being can truly be. We can make manifest substance of those thoughts that comes into our mind, the things that we hope for...even now.

Just using the faith or confidence that we have in our own natural abilities, we have the potential to do very amazing things. Imagine what is possible as we exercise our faith and trust in GOD our Father, and when we have better confidence and trust in Him to bring us more to the divine part of ourselves.

Just using the faith or confidence that we have in our own natural abilities, we have the potential to do very amazing things. Imagine what is possible as we exercise our faith and trust in GOD our Father, and when we have better confidence and trust in Him to bring us more to the divine part of ourselves.

We truly are made in our Father's image! Consider and imagine the things that are *humanly* attainable as faith sons and daughters of GOD when we attain *actionable* self-realization; actionable self-realization that makes manifest '*faith objects*' by being conditioned by the hope contained within our faith, based on truth and activated by our literal and practical works; and not just any kind of work, but the work that the Holy Spirit and the Spirit of GOD that dwells within us directs us to do.

The work, no matter how seemingly menial, nonsensical, or unrelated to the object to which faith is being directed may seem, it may be essential to receiving the hoped for and requested object. It may perhaps be some specific knowledge, or a particular attitude, mindset, belief system or behavior that must *first* be acquired and portrayed; or perhaps a skill that will be needed to acquire and be applied before, during or after receiving that which is the Father's Will to grant and give us. It will be something that will help maintain and sustain what He gives us in our package of prosperity.

Be certain of this! What the Father gives us and what we receive by faith, He *also* provides with it the *means* to maintain and sustain it and prepare us to do the greater works that Christ Jesus spoke to.

Human progression to perfection, to GOD likeness, is an ongoing process and faith in the Father, and faith in our abilities to apply the measure of faith given to us brings forth the 'divine you'. The divine you is concomitant with the acknowledgement and acceptance of GOD as our Heavenly Father and accepting Christ Jesus. For He was the incarnate person of Michael the Sovereign Master Creator Son of GOD. Then, as we realize and understand that the only way to the Father and His kingdom is through this Sovereign Son of GOD, and begin to acknowledge and truly believe that we are indeed and in truth a son or a daughter of this same GOD, He then ushers us into His kingdom and extends to us all that comes with that awesome and potentially everlasting gift.

THE CONFIRMATION OF TRUTH

> The Spirit of Truth enhances each person's ability to recognize truth. Its effectiveness is limited by each person's free-will consecration of his or her will to doing the Will of GOD, but its influence is Universal. When actively sought, the Spirit of Truth purifies the human heart and leads the individual to formulate a life purpose based on the love of truth.

Truths are confirmed as truth by the Spirit of Truth. He is the Spirit of Christ Jesus which was poured out on all flesh on the day of Pentecost; and this truth changes us gradually as our yearning for truth intensifies.

Making it personal, it changed me and continually inspires me to produce; motivating me to *progress* as only I can, and it will motivate you to progress as only *you* can.

The truth enables character traits that are spiritual in nature, qualities and values within you that over time develops your genuine spirituality; spirituality defined as being Christ like, having the mind of Christ; discovering (*seeking*), and then *living* the *religion practiced lived* by Christ Michael who was incarnated and bestowed in this world as Christ Jesus.

GOD the Eternal Son, the Second Source and Center is the Spirit gravity. Just as the force of gravity on planets pull and draws objects toward its' massive spherical body, so is GOD the Eternal Son, the Second GOD of the Paradise Trinity. Through GOD the Eternal Son all spirit is distributed to all beings throughout the Grand Universe and Master Universe of Their Creation. As He distributed His Spirit, He is also the Spirit gravity that draws all men unto Himself through Christ Michael's bestowal as a human being on this earth.

The things regarding *spirituality* are personal for each and every one of us as an individual. There is a Fragment of GOD the Universal Father that comes to dwell in every person at the time when they make their first moral choice. This Fragment of GOD indwelling us is how He knows our desires and needs as a person. Everything that we experience that is of *Spirit value for the Supreme Being*. Experiences that are of spirit value are our actions and thoughts dedicated to truth, beauty and goodness. The Supreme Being is the *evolving* GOD of experience, and He is the GOD that is the fourth Person of GOD the Sevenfold. He gathers into His repository the experiences of spirit value that will eventually be His character traits and personality. It is how He, GOD the Father knows us and how we come to know more of Him. His Spirit is your spirit, suited for the one of a kind…unique personality imparted to each of His children.

Your personality is that part of you that is…well…you! It is your soul! It is your personality, which shares the abode of your mind with the Spirit of and from GOD the Father, and through which a personal relationship expressly between the Father and each one of His children is maintained. It is sustained by our prayers, supplications and meditations that provide the medium to commune with Him always.

Christ Jesus is "the Way, the Truth, and the Life: No one comes to the Father but by Him." He is our inspiration to seek to be like our Father in Paradise and Christ Michael our local universe Father; for *He* was and *is* like the Father in Paradise. He reveals the Father to all who in spirit and truth seek to know Him. By seeking truth, recognizing beauty, portraying goodness, acknowledging the Fatherhood of GOD, and by receiving sonship and daughtership into His family in the kingdom of GOD, is how each person will survive this life and the life's to come after *this* mortal shell expires.

A new foundation of faith based upon truth is being laid; a foundation *not* build upon sand, for sand is porous. Having little firm substance, it will gradually give way and any solid matter which may be resting on its surface will sink. Whatever occupied that space will sink into despair and deprivation, and it will occupy that space no more.

This new foundation is built on rock. And not just any rock! It is the Rock of ages, the rock of truth, tried and true; and however slowly and tedious the *process* of the progression to perfection may be, brick by brick a new house, a new character, and a new behavior emerges from being preexistent *potential* to being potential existent to becoming *actual;* from the mind to literal reality.

We must eliminate the mindset that only certain people are qualified to teach us anything, and understand that truth and knowledge comes from a multitude of sources. It must! There are multitudes of people, multitudes of personalities and we must be willing to do whatever it takes and go whenever and wherever it is required as we are led by the Holy Spirit in order to discover truth, beauty, goodness and prosperity. We must know *when* the Spirit is leading us, discerning the particular manner by which He leads us as individual personalities.

This is part of the *personal spiritual experience;* and we *must* resolve within ourselves to obey! We obey by applying the truth that has been confirmed to us as truth; doing that which persists in our mind to do, and gradually coming to the spiritual state where the Fruit of the Spirit naturally enhances and enriches our life; at the same time enhancing and increasing our *spiritual reality* and giving us the power to become more the sons and daughters, enlightened children of GOD.

We must be objective; being able and willing to listen to, or read information with an open mind and give deliberate consideration to new information and not automatically reject the different and untraditional but factual and true information. Give credence to the sciences, philosophies and histories that might elicit greater insights into truth and *true* spiritual reality.

To Progress, we must discard much of the dogmatically held beliefs that so stubbornly resists and hinders one's spiritual growth; things which keep the object of our faith from being realized.

When you finally discard notions that even science has proven untrue, and which being a reasonable and logically rational human being you already had questions about, you are opening the door to begin the search for truth. You are ready for that Fragment of GOD who dwells within you, that Mystery Monitor who reveals the Heavenly Father to each truth seeking soul, causing them to begin His work of breaking the bonds of conformity, allowing you to see beyond the box in which ceremony, rituals and traditions have enslaved so many. Indeed, He begins to reveal the truth about Himself *and* all of the Heavenly hosts who do the Father's Will.

As you do open your mind your heart to the revelations that begins your journey to the truth, the truth that you discover will burst your bubble too. You will discover that there is a higher reality in which we as human beings and children of GOD are privileged to be part of. It is a reality that contains all of the *patterns* that are maintained in the archives of eternity; a pattern of all that we consider as life. You will come to realize that our reality is but a shadow of true reality, and that *all* patterns originate in the Universal Father, the First Source and Center of all things, material, spiritual and otherwise.

You will wonder why the messages you hear from the pulpits in churches of today, are only repetitious rhetoric which did not elicit understanding the first time, and it did not produce that real Spirit produced desire to tell someone about the truth you have discovered, if it was indeed the truth; because once the Spirit of Truth confirms that something is true, you become motivated to spread it like a wildfire controlled and pushed by the wind…with you being the igniter of the flames of truth.

The Spirit of Truth is not ambiguous and obscure in His answers to questions that are of a purely spiritual nature; questions that when asked, elicits an even deeper understanding and increases and reinvigorates faith. Sympathetically you realize that the truth you seek, that those who teach and preach traditional institutionalized religion, they cannot disclose because they do not know the reality of truly spiritual matters; and if they know it they are surely disinclined to reveal those truths to you, and for a very good reason.

It will not take long once you begin your journey until you begin having a new, a different and a profound appreciation for who our Heavenly Father truly is and *where* His kingdom truly is. As your mind grasps the depth of the revelations of truth being revealed, you will become awestruck and dwell less on temporal things and more on the spiritual things taking place in His kingdom…you become *born again!*

The Kingdom of GOD the Father is a kingdom of which *even now* we all are a part; because His kingdom is within our heart, our mind and everywhere else, whether we realize it, choose to acknowledge it, accept it and act on it or not.

You must be *observant* and *reflective:* Observant to discern confirmation that you are on the righteous path. The path on which, by faith, you believe and trust that you are being led into doing the Will of the Heavenly Father. Confirmation may come at any time and from anywhere, and you must be observant that it does not go without being received.

Confirmation of truth may come by means of a spiritual revelation giving you direction and guidance. Manipulated events and opportunities suddenly open up for you when you have taken the effort to discover seek the truth. It is a revelation that leaves no doubt that it is the course of action to take, or it may be the response to a specific question that you asked of the Father; especially in regard to how you should proceed, when you've asked what His Will is in the matter.

The revelation you received may be confirmed by someone that you meet who has been given a word of knowledge about the very subject matter of your interest, or who has had experience in the area of your interest. The revelation may confirm the uncertainty you have about a spiritual matter or clarify a dilemma that you were perhaps contemplating.

To confirm the answer revealed to you as the truth, or that it is the Will of the Father for you to pursue the course of action in response to the *existent potential* that the still small but persistent voice in your heart, is actually charting the course for you to pursue. It may come from someone with whom you share this revealed knowledge; who within a relatively short time, they too will have had a similar revelation of the truth regarding the same matter. You also serve as their confirmation of truth, giving both of you assurance, and confirming to them that they too are on the righteous path. Surely this has happened to you!

Verification of your *faith* may come by means of the door of *potential* opportunities suddenly opening; opportunities which may lead to the materialization of the object to which you have been *directing* your faith. A job offer may come from a *potential* employer with whom you have applied for employment months earlier, and that you had almost forgotten about. Suddenly they contact you for an interview. You get the job! And the *potential* employer becomes an *actual* employer.

Confirmation will always be related to a truth that has been revealed to you. *'That'* truth is the lesson to be learned and lived; to be applied in *like* manner the next time that you *direct* and *apply* your faith, actually exercising your faith, making it stronger and giving you more confidence and trust in GOD your Heavenly Father.

Give your faith direction. Applying it to an object that you need, or even desire to have. First seeking the Will of your Heavenly Father regarding the object, seeking to know whether or not it is His Will for you to have the object...whatever it may be.

Then, by faith, believe and trust that it is GOD's Will that the object be made manifest to you. Meditate on the object to which your faith is directed; and in your heart and in your mind believe and visualize that you have already received it.

By meditating on the object whether spiritual, physical, mental or material- you give a specific direction in which your faith is to be directed; and with the same faith, you first receive it mentally. Later in time, the means by which you are to attain or obtain the object of your faith becomes automatic because the process is being built on a solid foundation. It is the prerequisite process for *you* to receive the objects that GOD the Father desires you to have. The process that it will take for you to receive these objects will reveal itself to you as you are able to receive them, and as you become motivated to actually do what is required of you.

Always seek the truth, and seek to receive more understanding, knowledge and wisdom. Seek for better discernment of the truth and more spiritual endurance and stamina so that you will not be so distracted and weakened by the adversities that try to sway you from the true path, *your* true path.

It is a wise Proverb that says: "with all your getting get understanding." Although wisdom is the principle attribute and desired quality to possess, knowledge and understanding comes first. You must first get even cursory knowledge and understanding about the *process* of how a thing operates, how it works. A more defined process will soon reveal itself, breaking it down into its basic component parts, if necessary, for you to acquire knowledge and understanding.

Understanding comes by way of experience...your experience, and your experience is the truth for you; and from proven truth comes knowledge! Once you establish your experience as truth, for you it is the truth, if you get the same results every time that you perform an act, the process is repeatable, progressive and productive.

Then you *'know;'* and when that knowledge is applied, wisdom comes forth to produce prosperity.

Experience your truth, and in doing so, experience the truth of knowing the Lord our GOD as your Father in heaven; and at the same time, acknowledge and believe wholeheartedly that you are a faith son of GOD the First Person of the Paradise Trinity. For when you earnestly seek the kingdom of GOD, you can be certain that when once you enter His kingdom *all* these things will be added unto you.

Understand what Christ Jesus is saying! He said that; "all these things *shall* or *will* be added unto you." That means that they will be added whether you want them or not. The choice you have is whether you receive His bounties and blessings or not. It's a package deal!

It is GOD's Will that you accept Him as your Father in heaven... of this there can be no doubt! It is His Will that we come to know the truth about His true character and nature; that He is not a vengeful and wrathful GOD ready to impose punishment on the confused, misguided and misled population of a world He created by His Sovereign Son, Christ Michael. Instead, it is His Will for His children to look upon Him as He truly is; as a loving, caring and giving Father who delights in seeing His children progress by faith, seeing His created human beings progressing to perfection by our persistent efforts to be like him.

When you seek the kingdom of GOD, you are automatically seeking His righteousness. You become more responsible in managing the 'all' that comes with it. That's part of the process of teaching us how to maintain and sustain what He gives us. And the 'all' is meant to benefit you and to benefit others through you. When we accept and receive son or daughter-ship of the First Source and Center, GOD the Seven fold Father, you do have power as a son or daughter of His.

The *power* you receive is at first just potential, but then, as you increase your faith by earnestly declaring that, "*your* will is that *His Will* be done in your life" and in the world; and as you increasingly trust that it is His Will that you know Him, in deed and in time, you will come to appreciate a personal relationship with the Father that only you can experience. And He will give you power, the likes of which nothing on this or any other world can compare.

You must be *reflective*, because you must always review your past experiences with careful contemplation to understand where you have been and what happened at different points along your journey. Make an honest objective personal assessment to try to grasp where the Spirit has been leading you up to this point, and why? And when the veil has been lifted from your mind's eyes and it most certainly will be lifted then you will discover a definite method, a pattern in your life that repeats itself. It is the method that applies to *your* life's purpose and reveals the direction in which you should proceed to fulfill that purpose and prosper. Follow that path. For that is the way in which your indwelling GOD Fragment your Thought Adjuster and the Holy Spirit leads *you* specifically and uniquely. They are leading you on a path that is common *only* to you. This is a major part of *your personal relationship* with the Father.

Faith is conditional. It is first and foremost, conditioned by your belief, by your trust and confidence in GOD the Heavenly Father; that He is your Father and that you are His son or daughter. As a child trusts and believes in their human parents, you can and should have much more belief, confidence and trust in your Heavenly Father. Even when the human father or mother is absent from the child, the Heavenly Father never abandons you. He loves you unconditionally with a love and devotion unimaginable and never ending.

But also, faith is conditioned by whether or not your request is in accordance with the W*ill* of GOD the Universal Father; that the requested object of your faith is what *He* wants you to have. Will it produce spirit value attributes, character and actions that assist in your progression to perfection? For that surely is His Will for all of His beings with ascension potential. Or will it engender undesirable behavior and character that is unsuitable for one of His children? A nurturing parent does not encourage undesirable behavior by enabling it to continue; giving those whom He has given divine purpose things that would cause them to go astray…unless it is a lesson being taught…and there are many lessons to be learned.

Then there's the condition which requires *work*; physical and or mental activity or exertion; the activation of potential energy and the incitement of the kinetic energy you are capable of producing. As it is prompted by the indwelling Spirit, your path is revealed by the Mystery Monitor, the Spirit of GOD the Father who dwells within you. The energy you expend will produce the desired outcome. There are hosts of unseen beings manipulating events, directing and guiding us, helping us make correct choices. The Seraphic Guardians of Destiny are angels protecting us in our ascension as well as other ministering Spirits who guide us on our journey through this uncertain maze called life.

The *work* is the *persistent* activity directed toward your obtaining the requested object of your faith that you have petitioned the Heavenly Father for. The work may be those things that from time to time we are unexplainably driven and motivated to do, albeit subconsciously. But most assuredly, faith is conditioned by prayers and supplication of sincere thanksgiving with the earnest expectation of receiving the faith object petitioned.

It is further conditioned by meditation; allowing our soul, our personality to commune with the Spirit of GOD the Father dwelling within us; but it is also conditioned by meditating on the object of our desire or need as well.

When these conditions are met, and even while in the process, in time, in GOD's own time, and if it is His Will and always pray that *it is* His Will then, as you are ready to receive it, strengthening of your belief and trust in the Father will occur and enable your faith to increase when you do attain or obtain that which now '*was*' the object of your faith. And you will be overwhelmed with joy; not only by the personal one-on-one relationship that you now *know* you have with the Universal Father, but by an ever increasing and natural display of the Fruit of the Spirit in your life.

When the spiritual, physical and even material things for which you have been *praying, meditating* and *working* for materializes into existence, becoming manifest for all to witness, the thing itself will be of little importance in comparison to the assurance and confidence that the *experience* of truly knowing GOD as your loving Father excites within you. You will not only *want* to share your personal spiritual experiences, but you will also have the *need* to share them...and you invariably will!

When you establish a relationship with the Father, you will begin to portray the attributes of a faith son of GOD, the beginning of the progressing sons and daughters we are ultimately to become... you should start practicing now. As you do, you will undoubtedly discover, that the reward is not always in the treasure you find at the *end* of the journey, it is the journey itself, the search...the seeking and in the discoveries, you make along the way. It requires courage to embark on adventures into uncharted territory, not knowing what situations, perils and what treasures you may encounter along the way.

Think of the joy you receive when at last along the path of your journey to perfection, you discover a nugget of extreme value. You have found some of what you've been searching for, working so hard for and suffering for so long to attain or obtain. And going further still, maybe days or years distant, you discover a nugget of even more value…nuggets of truth! Worth much more than gold!

Nevertheless, you should be aware and understand that many a journey is fraught with danger and obstacles, and sometimes with pain, suffering and sorrow; but these are the ways of life, these things would happen anyway! You are being prepared to survive the journeys in *this* life *and* in your others. No one is immune! To view life from the perspective that these things add spice to the experiences we have in life, makes difficult experiences much easier to contend with.

It just depends upon how we view *our* life in particular and all of life in general. It all begins with us hoping to become the person we aspire to be. To whom do you compare yourself? Who or what is the main object of your affection? What floats your boat? Who is at the helm of the ship in your life? Who or what is your source of strength? Who or what motivates or drives you to continue in your pursuits? Do you have the confidence, the assurance, and especially the knowledge however basic it may be at this point that regardless of what happens to you in this life, that it is the Father's Will for you and that it *is* for your good?

Life *is* an adventure and that thought process helps us endure life's little and not so little traumas when we view it *as* an adventure. It is an adventure in which each day that we live there will be problems to solve and situations with which to contend. There will be pleasant and good days as well as days you wish had never happened. And as long as we live, there will always be issues.

Some may *seem* overwhelming at times, and try the very limits of your patience, endurance and even your sanity. It is those times when you must deal with difficult issues that make the small issues appreciated.

Yet even in the *process* of contending with these issues, there are experiences to be had, and with the experience there is knowledge to be gained and understood; there is wisdom to be obtained and faith to be applied, practiced and deployed, and objects of faith to be made manifest. Along the way, prosperity is assured as you repeat the process of applying what has been learn; this is the *practical application* of faith...this is living *by* faith!

Faith based upon truth is the divining instrument that uncovers the nuggets of prosperity spiritual, physical, mental and material prosperity. It is by faith that we accept and receive sonship as a faith son or daughter of the Paradise Father.

But lest you receive a mistaken concept of the purpose of faith, and indeed, even misinterpret what faith truly is, this explanation is given that you understand this concept of faith; according to *my* understanding of what faith is and how it is deployed to bring forth what we desire.

Spiritual Faith is first and foremost our self-discovery of GOD the Father; the acknowledgment and acceptance of, and the wholehearted belief and trust in GOD as our Heavenly Father. It is receiving son-ship or daughter-ship of GOD and having the understanding that as His child, we too have the capacity to be even as Christ Jesus was; being both human and divine. The love for the Father and for humanity serves to motivate and compel us to keep seeking truth, to keep working in His kingdom through the constant application of our faith, using faith to create the things that benefit both humankind and that benefit you and yours as well.

Though the Kingdom of GOD, the Kingdom of heaven is in our heart once we acknowledge GOD and we accept and receive son or daughter-ship, the amount that the Kingdom is in our heart is quantified by our commitment to knowing and doing the Father's Will; commitment that elicits the attributes that Michael the Master Creator Son portrayed in His magnificent bestowal life on earth as Christ Jesus of Nazareth. Such a life is attainable by faith for all those who aspire to ascend to those levels of spirituality; those who seek truth, acknowledges beauty and practices goodness!

Having faith in yourself has its merits and its rewards. Believing in yourself and your abilities, and having confidence and trust in yourself often produces no less than a comfortable living experience and lifestyle, and yet it may still not be the Will of the Father for that person. What He allows and what is His Will are not always synonymous. Our Father desires that we live the life that we can based upon our station in life; the environments in which we are born into.

The Father loves us enough to not interfere in the affairs of mankind and to let us progress by the natural course of events as they unfold, to evolve as they will. Our Father has faith! He is Faith Personified! He knows that in due time, humanity will progress to the state of Light and Life that they are destined to attain and enjoy; He has ordained it to be so!

While the perpetual applying of faith is the only acceptable means to gain access to the kingdom of heaven, and a powerful and wonderful tool by which to bring to this physical world the things that are spiritual, faith is not a personal possession to be taken for granted once its process of application is discerned. Faith is not to be deployed as a means to obtain objects totally for self-gratification through the acquirement of wealth and material stuff. It is to be employed in the fulfillment of our physical, material and most of all spiritual needs. It is to be employed in the fulfillment of the needs of the brotherhood and sisterhood of humankind, and to provide a reasonable amount of comfort from the hardships of life for ourselves and for others.

Personally, I keep finding precious gems of truth along the path of *my* journey. Using the *measure of faith* that has been apportioned to *me*, applying faith as it has been revealed to me and perceived by me as the method by which *I* am to apply *my* measure of faith for practical living and spiritual growth. And when I comply with the guidance, I am receiving from my indwelling GOD Fragment, the objects of my *directed faith* keep being manifested. The truths to support my beliefs continue being confirmed and becoming a part of *my* personal spiritual experience.

You too will surely receive inspiration, encouragement and reinforcement by the *confirmations* and object manifestations you receive. The revelations that you receive you may initially perceive as just a passing thought or only as a brief passing notion, but then, there comes the Mystery Monitor, who unceremoniously asserts a notion which persists in your heart in your very soul, and it will not release its mild but never aggressive intrusive hold on your mind. You will come to perceive and experience these relentless notions or thoughts as revealed truths or direction; giving guidance in finding the door of opportunity that is open or must be opened in readiness for you to experience what lies within.

The truth that lies within may not be immediately acted upon or even come to your awareness for a period of time, but when it does and you act on it, you will have a peace of mind that you cannot understand. This peace you will enjoy even when your directed action is something that causes the loss of a material possession, or something that may later cause you to have to endure initial trauma, taking you out of your comfort zone. This is the peace that surpasses all understanding.

Don't be distressed, become afraid or begin to doubt. In due time, you will be given assurance, understanding and knowledge as a revelation, confirming that what you have discovered and what must be endured is indeed truth. The Spirit of Truth and the ministering spirits are confirming that the action you have taken is in fact the proper action, and that you are proceeding in the direction in which you should proceed. Be confident in it!

FAITH AND HOW IT IS APPLIED

E very since the concept of faith was introduced to human kind, we have grappled with the notion of what faith actually is, not being really sure of just what faith does, or what it's for. Most people don't have a clue as to how it is applied in their spiritual life, not to mention its application in everyday life. People seem to consider faith as merely believing something that has no physical, visible or material means of being verified; and this *is* a *form* of faith as long as it has its basis in truth.

For many in the clergy and lay persons as well, faith is used as a crutch; a means to squelch questions about religion or scripture that a curious and bewildered person may have; answers to questions the minister either doesn't know, or to which they are not inclined to divulge to the curious person…for whatever reason. The curious congregant may often be told; "Oh, there now dear brother (sister) you just gotta' have faith! Some things in scripture you just gotta' take on faith, and not let it bother you…"

Imagine having a congregation that knows what faith is and who actually applies faith based on the precepts of *truth*. Ministers and preachers would be out of a job!

I pose these simple questions: If ministers and those in the clergy were teaching faith precepts based on truth, then why are there relatively few who actually *receive* what they are asking of GOD? And if people, those who profess to be Christians were applying truth-based faith according to divine precepts, then why are there so many prosperity deprived people in this world?

No…prosperity is not for everyone! But it is for those to whom it is GOD's Will that they be prosperous. Many don't have prosperity. But it's not because they lack the faith, because it takes very little to move mountains, but rather because they have not yet learned how to apply and direct their faith toward the object of their need or desire; a need or desire which the Father wants them to have.

It's simple! The institutional religious doctrine of faith being taught and being attempted but not effectively applied today is without *substance*; substance less doctrine lacks the power to make manifest the requested object, much less the desires of their heart. If the supposed faith is without substance, having neither spiritual nor practical value then it is not faith. It is wishful thinking at best.

According to Biblical scripture, *"faith* is the *substance* of things *hoped* for, the *evidence* of things not seen. Okay! But what does that mean? The *thing(s)*, the *object(s)* you *hope* for provides the *substance* of faith; it is the *object* of your faith, albeit as yet only potentially existent, because it now only exists in your mind as a shadow of the reality that is to come...should it be GOD's Will. The material thing may already exist somewhere, and in truth it already does exist if only in the Being of GOD the First Source and Center. But it is not yet yours as a material possession, which is where your *genuine* faith and the will of GOD will place it in due time...in your material possession.

Hope is defined as: "something good that you want to happen in the future; or a confident feeling about what will happen in the future." It is this confident feeling, your expectancy which stimulates your faith. The amount of hope, belief and trust that you engender is what motivates you and prompts you into action.

First, you must believe that faith *works* and can make the object of your requests become a reality in your life experience. Faith must then be acknowledged as being faith. You must be consciously aware that you are using faith; even proclaiming to GOD the Father that by faith your hope is that the object be made manifest and come to fruition... *if* it is His Will. And always pray that it is His Will.

If you don't believe that you will receive the object, why hope for it? The substance gives faith direction, providing faith with a purpose and releasing the knowledge, by way of revelations from the Spirit of GOD within you, as to how you should proceed; knowledge that is necessary for the substance to become manifest.

Hope provides the earnest expectation, your most sincere belief that what you asked for, you have already received...by faith. And then it's just a matter of coming to the receiving point in time; the point in time when you actually *receive* the object of your faith.

Don't despair! It may seem as though there is no benefit from the effort that you've been exerting, and the work that you have been performing to bring the object of your faith to manifestation seems fruitless, and the object that your faith has been directed toward seems as far away now as it was in the beginning. Do not give in to the temptation to doubt that you will receive what is your Heavenly Father's will to give you.

Substance is defined as: "the real part or element of anything; the unchanging essence of something, reality." It is also; "the physical matter of which a thing is made, that which is material;" meaning that, it is perceivable with the senses." But it is also: "The real content of a statement; the true meaning."

The things that you hope for are real. You hope for things that are material; the things that have substance which you can touch, see, taste, smell and hear. But you also hope for things that the physical senses cannot detect; things which the mind however *does* perceive, things such as knowledge, understanding, wisdom and love, truth, beauty and goodness. The mind uses the functions of the brain to coordinate the actions that you take.

When you apply faith based upon true concepts and precepts, directing your faith to the receiving of higher moral character, GOD like character the fruit of the Spirit then the Spirit of GOD the Father who dwells within your mind begins to gradually alter your attitude, thought processes and behavior. You will begin to portray those qualities naturally, and not as some pretentious self willed act.

These things have substance as well, just of a different nature; of a spiritual nature which has spirit value and practical use in our everyday living experiences.

They have true meaning and even more value because they are perceived by your spirit, the Fragment of GOD the Father who resides within your mind, and you continue to be stimulated by the belief and trust that your actions are indeed in synch with the Will of the Father.

Trust in the Heavenly Father completely, wholeheartedly, and believe that the actions that you take are those that you are being led to do; that they are the required components or ingredients that *you* are to provide to make the conditions favorable for you to receive your faith object. Have confidence and truly believe that you have received it already…in time; even to the point of visualizing yourself with the needed or desired object, or seeing in your mind the person who needs healing, being actually healed, and so on.

Visualization is a part of the *meditation process*. The more that you meditate the better you will be able to discern the leading of the Ministering Spirit, the teaching and comforting of the Holy Spirit, and the mysteries of GOD the Father as they are revealed by His Spirit already dwelling in your mind. And when you meditate to receive spiritual prosperity in the form of more knowledge, understanding, and wisdom and an abundance of the Fruit of the Spirit, the more apt you become in performing the activities that produce these attributes and character traits within yourself.

We live in a material and physical world, and things that you see as well as those things you can't actually witness by sensual perception, they also have substance. Those things exist but in the spiritual realm where the *pattern* of the thing you are hoping for originates.

It is through the persistent applying of faith that you receive the object of your faith; going through the required process of declaring in your request that the Father's Will be done in the matter at hand and in the reception of your faith object. And again, always pray that the object of your faith petition is His Will.

Faith is the means of the '*power*' that the sons and daughters of GOD possess, though latent it may be. It only awaits it's awakening in you by the realization that the kingdom of GOD is within you, and that since you have entered His kingdom, all of these things are added unto you.

Do not be so proud as to deny yourself all that your Paradise Father has for you. You must literally humble yourself and *ask* the Father for what it is you need or desire in your heart then believe and trust in Him to bring the object to manifestation by your works. It is a divine partnership!

Oftentimes extreme confidence in something, especially your spiritual beliefs, can give people -who don't have a clue as to your personal relationship with GOD the Father the false impression that you are arrogant and prideful, but it is only your faith-filled assurance, confidence and belief that His Will shall be done in the matter.

Believe! Believe so much that you thank Him constantly before hand. And then direct your faith; meditate often on the object so that the door of opportunity will be revealed and opened to you. Meditate to reveal the means and the method that is required for you to apply the practical actions you should perform; and pray and meditate for the supplies and the resources you will need to perform your part of the manifestation process. Then wait for the Spirit of GOD to reveal the door(s) that you must *knock* on and allow to open, and anticipate the work or effort that you will almost automatically be inclined to do. Those works are the things which in time will *actually* make manifest your requested object.

Once the object has been made manifested, it the object itself provides the evidence of your faith. And now faith turns to assurance that all you have experienced was indeed and in truth, the will of the Father.

You can have the assurance of the Father's Will and the assurance that you will receive the object even before making the request of the Father by removing all doubt that He will provide for you, and by eliminating all fear that anything that is not the Will of the Father will befall you.

Yes, there will be times when you wonder if the Father is even hearing you, and you will sometimes give in to a season of questioning and reluctance to act because you see no *evidence* forthcoming. You may become more circumspect with regard to your actions, and this you should do!

But don't despair! There are things going on behind the scenes that relate directly or indirectly to bringing to fruition the object of your faith. Super intelligent beings and personalities of the Heavenly host are performing the functions in which they specialize to help make the requested object a material and real manifestation in your life's experience.

That unseen thing now becomes manifest and perceivable with your physical senses. The object is now the *evidence*, the proof that *faith* was employed in bringing the *hoped for object* the object itself in whatever form to fruition.

In a court of law, the prosecuting attorney must produce evidence to substantiate their claim about the guilt of a suspected offender. Likewise, the defense attorney must also provide evidence to the contrary in order to refute the prosecutor's claim. Once this evidence is admitted and accepted by the judge, then the attorneys can elaborate about what the evidence supposedly provides; proving that certain conditions existed whereby only the defendant could be guilty of committing the act, or else the evidence acts to vindicate the accused of the offense.

Aside from the precepts of faith, which is mostly that your faith is based on the foundation of and your belief in the truth and your earnest expectation of receiving your requested object, you must acknowledge the Universal Father as the Source of the object, and believe that the measure of faith that you possess is sufficient to accomplish what you are asking to receive from the Father. You must trust Him unconditionally to give you the object to which you are directing your faith, if it is His Will to do so. Again...pray that it is His Will!

But *understand* what you are asking for! You are asking for the Paradise Trinity, the Universal Father, the First Source and Center, through GOD the Eternal Son, and by whatever means that GOD the Infinite Spirit may employ to bring the object of your faith to fruition. This means that you are willing to endure whatever you must in order for you to secure and obtain the requested object. And this means that you are asking for the Heavenly Father to prepare you to receive His marvelous gift, the object of your faith.

It is very likely that you will immediately begin experiencing phenomenon in your life that you may initially perceive as hardships, trials or tribulations; otherwise known as adversities, but you may just as immediately experience relief from some physical or material and certainly spiritual burden. In these cases, you may have already endured your time of preparation, and it's now a matter of reflecting over the past events of your life to discover the lesson(s) that the Father has diligently sought to teach you. And when you discover and apply His lessons to your life, then *receive* your requested faith object.

This is the case many times! What you have asked for has already been granted and given to you but you haven't received it... yet! There will always be something that you must do that directly relates to your obtaining what you have asked for.

As an example: You have prayed and by supplication asked the Father for a house, and you meditate regularly, focusing on and visualizing yourself in a house, a home of your own. And then, almost immediately you begin experiencing issues or problems with the house or apartment in which you currently reside. Then to add to your frustration your neighbors begin causing you considerable irritation and bringing continuous annoyances to your life.

The Holy Spirit, and the Seraphic Guardians of Destiny, your destiny, are manipulating events and directing you with prompts that urge you to take specific actions. But you delay because your credit is bad, or you don't have the money necessary to make a move, or you're simply *afraid* to step outside of your comfort zone and experience the unknown. You're reluctant and nearly paralyzed at the thought of leaving the things to which you have become accustomed; one reason so many creative and intelligent people don't progress and prosper.

Nevertheless, you keep hoping! But hoping is not enough! You must perform work; doing the thing(s) that your indwelling GOD Fragment and the Holy Spirit urges you to do; the thing(s) that persistently and relentlessly occupies your conscious and even your subconscious mind, instructing you, and directing you in what actions to perform and which path you should take. And they the celestial beings and Ministering Spirits of the Heavenly hosts await your decision and action(s).

You will always have choices to make and you must choose wisely, allowing events to unfold and show you the way. And then when you respond and do what is required, and as you trust and believe that it is the Father's Will that you do those things, whatever they may be, then you are acting and living by faith. And the Father recognizes it as faith and responds in kind. This then becomes your personal *spiritual* experiences.

DESTROYERS OF THE MANIFESTATION OF YOUR FAITH OBJECTS

Now you have gone to church regularly as if that matters; you have prayed fervently, and you have done everything that you know to do, trying to obtain the object(s) that you so much need or desire. Yet the objects' manifestation eludes you, and you wonder why. In frustration and perplexity, you ask...what am I doing wrong GOD? Why are you not giving me what you know that I need or desire? And then another state of mind comes over you. You begin to doubt! Questioning or wondering if there truly is a GOD? And if there is, does He truly answer prayers? And if He does, why doesn't He answer yours? Now, anxiety and fear begin to overwhelm you and you wonder if He is punishing you for something you've done or haven't done. And your fear leads to dread and ultimately to despair and hopelessness, and without hope, just the same as without works, your faith is dead.

You will invariably encounter doubt and fear which you must immediately discard from your mind through meditation and prayer to overcome. These negatively charged elements seek to rob you of the nutrients provided by your hopes, and if allowed to continue they will erode the foundation of truth that you obtained by trusting in the Father to keep His Word. They subtly steal the belief that you have; that He *will* supply your needs.

In the shadows of confidence, courage and trust lurks low self-esteem, *doubt* and *fear*. They are always close at hand, seeking the slightest opportunity to inject themselves into the mix and displace your trust, and make ineffective your faith. It may be superficial at first, but over time if you relent and give in to doubt and fear, allowing your mind to continually dwell on how GOD *didn't* do something, rather than giving Him thanks for all that He *has* done and that He is doing and that He will do, then the roots of these destroyers of faith will firmly take hold and become increasingly more difficult to uproot.

GOD our Father is 'not' a GOD to be feared! Yes, the Bible especially the Old Testament is replete with commands to *fear* GOD. But you should be aware and understand that although well intentioned, the prophets and people issuing those commands were of a primitive mind. The concept of one GOD had not been firmly established in the hearts and minds of the people of those times. And fear was a method, then, as it is even today that was used to gain the control and obedience of the people.

Notwithstanding, the word *fear* was also used in the context of putting their trust and having trust in GOD. You should be able to discern the difference. Nowhere in the four Gospels of the New Testament will you find where Christ Jesus sought to use fear tactics to compel or make people believe and trust in GOD the Father. Indeed, He sought to dispel people's fears about the Heavenly Father being a GOD of vengeance and wrath, and replace those binding fears with the truth of His unconditional love, and His caring and nurturing attributes and character. It was and still is Christ Jesus' method of *persuading* people to accept GOD as their Heavenly Father; by telling them the truth so that they could indeed and in truth be made free. To use fear tactics or any kind of tactic to make someone do something against their will truly undermines the Father's basic precept of free will. If a person is being made, compelled to do a thing, then is that thing which they are compelled to do by their own will? I don't think so! That is to impose spiritual bondage upon people. And above all else, it was a desire of Christ Jesus to make them free and to lift them out of their spiritual bondage.

Although doubt and fear are the two most detrimental elements to our faith and our faith object's manifestation, there are numerous other faith negating attitudes that preclude, prevent your faith from being productive and coming to fruition.

Personal idiosyncrasies like disbelief, envy, jealousy and greed are but a few more character traits, attitudes of mind and acts of behavior that diminish your capacity to apply the measure of faith apportioned to you. What reason have you to be envious, or jealous or greedy when you have the ability and capacity by faith to have all that is in the Father's storehouse that is meant just for you? You have not come to realize your own inherent potential.

Portraying those negative traits are an indication that you don't know who you truly are; neither as your own person, nor as a son or daughter of your Heavenly Father. Trying to be someone else, someone other than yourself, is the motive that drives those attitudes and their resulting behaviors; and they are *not* conducive to you *ever* acquiring that which is GOD the Father's Will for you to have.

GOD, your Heavenly Father has allowed those whom you envy or that you are jealous of, to have what they have for reasons of His own and should not be questioned; for to question why they are so privileged is to dwell on the possessions they have, rather than to meditate on the means to obtain what the Father has for you. Many of them have acquired what they have through no spiritual effort of their own, having obtained them through inheritance, through their own abilities or by unscrupulous means; and the latter is certainly not the will of GOD. However *allowing* them to have prosperity or wealth could serve as an inspiration for others.

Be encouraged and apply your measure of faith to obtain the things that are for you. And you won't know until you set aside those negative and faith limiting attitudes and behaviors and apply your faith. The degree of prosperity that is for you, in time and by faith will be yours for the asking and receiving.

LIFE'S SEASONS

To understand how faith is applied, you must begin to understand the basic precepts of faith, and more so, the process by which faith operates. There is one you know…a process. *A process is*; "a series of *actions directed toward a specific aim!*" Practically everything, if not everything has a process by which it operates. *You* have a process by which *you* operate. Your process of operation is defined within your personality and stimulated by the Spirit of GOD that dwell within your mind.

So, it begins with a thought within your mind. A perceived need, desire or want, and your mind dwells on that thought until it begins to form a concept about a way to make material the picture image you have now conceived. Then the desire to acquire the substance represented by that picture image if the desire is strong enough- motivates you to do something that may invariably bring that desired object or object of need into your material reality; or it demoralizes and de-motivates you causing you to do nothing. Thus, the process begins.

The process is reflected by the deliberate actions that you take based on the choices which you decide to implement. These choices govern your actions and produce the same repetitious result when having to make choices in the future when you have needs or desires of a similar nature, or when you encounter similar circumstances or events.

It seems that many people are not even aware of or consider that all of their actions have consequences, and sometimes undesirable consequences that result from the choices made. They have little insight into how their actions affects their life and the lives of others. Many others are aware of the consequences of their actions but choose to perform the action regardless of the consequence to themselves or to their fellow human beings.

Our daily life is full of processes but we seldom realize it because they are a matter of routine. There are certain things that we become accustomed to doing and things that we absolutely refuse to do; it matters not whether it positively or negatively affects our life. Still, the brain functions as the *processing* center for all the activities that we perform; those things become o*ur will* put into motion.

Yet that force, that spirit within us, stimulates and motivates us to perform the processes that are in accordance with the will of GOD the Father. And it is those processes that invariably determine how we view life in general and *our* life specifically; and more importantly, the processes by which we live our life determines the extent to which we progress spiritually and indicates how prepared we are to receive the object(s) of our faith, the objects of our prayers and supplications.

As concerning the precepts of faith, the process by which faith operates, consider and understand the concept of sowing and reaping. Everything happens in its season and the Heavenly Father does not interfere with the natural order or the natural unfolding of events in the natural course of time in which they would normally occur.

That being said…if it is the Will of the Paradise Father, then seasons can be either shorter or longer, just as the weather seasons vary in length of time as a natural course of events. But that is the Father's domain! Ours is to learn to live by faith and learn the seasons of our lives, and adjust our activities and life patterns in accordance with the season at each point of our life. And there is no conflict between the seasons of our life and our fulfilling the will of GOD.

When once the Will of the Father is known through the Ministering Spirits, the Seraphic Guardians of Destiny, the Cherubim and others assigned to guide, direct and protect you, these beings of the Heavenly host busy themselves making the will of GOD come to pass in its due season.

Though you may not know what the Father's Will is for you, you proceed as though your actions are His Will. And in meditative thanksgiving, internally or vocally, receive the objects of your faith in the name of Christ Jesus / Christ Michael. Receiving them by the ways and means of your indwelling GOD Fragment and the Holy Spirit. This is *a* means of *directing* your faith, giving your faith direction and allowing the Divine Minister of the universe and her ministering spirits to bring it to fruition.

There is a lot mentioned in Scripture about '*seasons,*' and that's for a very good reason. Things happen in *their* season! You wouldn't plant or sow seeds in the dead of winter. The conditions are not favorable for them to grow and produce fruit. Instead, you begin cultivating the ground in late fall, winter or early spring the *cultivating season* preparing the ground to receive the seeds you want to sow.

You need not think that the work of cultivating the ground is always something physically exerting. It is not! It can just as likely be mental preparation as well as something physically demanding; preparing your heart, your mind and your body to be in a discerning and receptive state wherein you can recognize the fertile ground from the infertile, so you can begin to sow the seeds of prosperity.

Next, comes the *sowing* season. You begin sowing the seeds. The seeds are the services you perform for your fellow brothers and sisters of humanity. The seeds are also your sincere and fervent prayers and supplications to the Father for what you need, the *objects of your faith*, your desires.

In spirit and in truth you begin praying, and in supplication to the Father, being persistent in *asking* Him for what you *need*; and in worshipful meditation, communing with the Father, seeking to discern and know His Will in the matter. You begin envisioning the object(s) that you are hoping to receive. And through meditation, in your mind you receive those objects by wholeheartedly believing that it is the Heavenly Father's Will that you receive them. Internally acknowledging that the LORD GOD has already given it to you, and thanking Him for His gift(s) even though they may not be *actual* as yet.

Listen for your indwelling Spirit to direct you in what *work* you need to do, and then perform the task(s) when it is confirmed that this *is* indeed what the Spirit is directing you to do. Sometimes you can't be sure, because that persistent urge in your head instructing you to do something may be your own ego. Sometimes the actions that the Spirit wants you to perform seems to have nothing to do with what you are asking, but do it anyway.

There are no mistakes! Romans 8:28... remember? "*All* things work together for the good."

However, you can be sure that His Will embraces all that is truth, beauty and goodness, and the indwelling Spirit is not going to direct you to do anything that goes against GOD's Laws of truth, justice and righteousness. So let this be your motivator: "*All things* work together for good to them who love GOD; to them who are the called according to His purpose." This is why we are to rejoice and thank Him for all things, for this is the will of GOD in Christ Jesus concerning us.

If you are applying and practicing faith based on truth, and if you are asking for *His Will* to be done in the matter, then you *are* called according to *His* purpose and you can rest in the assurance of hope and in the comforting of the Holy Spirit, that you are proceeding in accordance with His Will. You are a son or daughter of GOD the Father in heaven...you should behave like it by applying and exercising your faith.

It is not a practice in faith to endeavor to bargain with the Heavenly Father. That is an exercise in futility! What does anyone of us have to offer GOD our Father except our love, devotion, loyalty, worship, and praise, and the giving of our services in the spiritual development of brotherhood to our fellow human beings?

And we must do all of *these* in *spirit* and in *truth.*

Everything that we have comes from GOD the First Source and Center. We have *nothing* to bargain with! The Universal Father is going to do what His Will dictates that He does. The everlasting part of His Will is to love and care for all of His created beings, whether they are spiritual, morontia, or mortal. And regardless of anything you or anybody else does to prevent it, what is His Will for you, is meant for you and you only; but you must receive it by faith.

You need not be overly concerned about the situations or circumstances that you have to endure or that you are enduring; particularly since what He does *is* for your good, whether you think so at the moment or not. Endure for as long as you can and be longsuffering. Your Heavenly Father knows how much you can bear. Through His Creator Son Christ Michael He made you, and He knows that His human beings have a great capacity for endurance. And when you can no longer endure things *will* change! All things in time *come* to *pass*! That's the nature of time and the natural course of human progression to perfection...at least progression toward perfection to the degree that anyone can attain in their mortal life.

Along with listening be *observant*, be *vigilant* and watch for opportunities that will inevitably present themselves. Watch and wait for doors to open as you knock. It is written that Christ Jesus said: "*Ask* and it *shall* be given you, *seek* and you *shall* find, '*knock*' and it *shall* be opened unto you."

Do exactly what Christ say's to do: *ask, seek,* and *knock*…literally! Find a door and knock on it, several times. There is nothing superstitious or mysterious about it, it's simply following directions in the *process* of receiving. If you don't knock on the door, how will opportunity know that you're there seeking entrance and open unto you the adventure and maybe even the *actual* treasure you seek?

Yes, it sounds silly! A lot of things do to materially minded people attempting to encounter and experience spiritual things; people who are trying to capture spiritual *realities* without understanding the truth. Besides, if one is so skeptical, reserved and negligent about doing the smallest task, how much less likely will one be to perform the more serious tasks required for their object to be made manifest? Look! You literally do the first two directives; *you ask* and *you seek*…why not literally do the third as well? Why don't you knock? It does work!

Then comes the *growing* season. The seeds that you have sown begin to grow, and in a relatively short period of time begin to produce fruit. The key words are *time* and relatively. The seeds produce fruit relative to the amount of time required for all of the conditions to be met and for faith to run its course and come to fruition for the particular seeds you have planted.

But along with the fruit producing plants, weeds also grow and come up along with the desired fruit. The weeds try to take root and deprive the fruit producing plants of the nutrients necessary for them to bare their fruit in their season. The weeds are the religious fallacies, the temptations, the trials, tribulations, and all the unproductive things that we may allow our mind to dwell upon, as well as the negatively charged and unproductive things we do.

When you realize, understand and practice the process of applying faith, then the belief that you have will become and remain strong during the period of your preparation to receive the objects of your faith. You will not become angry with the Father for delaying His gift to you. You will be more prone to *search within yourself* for the revelation of what it is the Father -through Christ Jesus and His Spirit of Truth and the Holy Spirit- is attempting to teach you.

In earnest, you begin to acknowledge and accept the condition your mind and heart is currently in; and in genuine sincerity you are gradually propelled to the state of humility that must be present in your life so that He may give you the things for which you have asked; the things that will not cause you harm or harm to others. Then when He gives you the desires of your heart, you will remain loyal to Him and be even more confident and trusting of Him. Most of all, He is preparing you to acknowledge Him as the 'One' from whom came the object(s) of your faith; and in your gratitude you show your appreciation by giving Him *glory, honor* and *praise* for His infinite Love and over care for you and for all of His creation.

Now comes the *harvest*. Your crops have weathered the storms and you have endured the experience of applying your faith, the preparation period. You have discerned the revelations of knowledge, and through experience you have come to understand the spiritual reality associated with the manifestation of the objects of your faith. You have gained wisdom through these experiences and have begun to apply the precepts learned from that wisdom. Now the produce is ready to be picked and harvested. All along you have been working, doing that which was necessary for the object of your faith the crop that you have planted to grow and produce fruit. It has now been made manifest. Your faith has come to fruition, but a little more work is yet to be done.

The fruit must be plucked from the vine, and some preserved, some must be stored, and much of it must be shared. The finishing touches must be applied to maintain that which you have so diligently sought and worked for, and which has now come to fruition so that you may have food during the interim periods, both in and out of season.

Go to the realtor and apply for that house! And when you do, much to your surprise and satisfaction you find that your credit is not as bad as you thought, and you are preapproved for the loan to purchase your own home. Now you search for the house that the Father has prepared for you and you find it and complete the necessary paperwork to finalize the deal.

You will discover that it is not so much the fruit that comes from the plant, albeit that too, but the greater joy comes from the experience that you have gained, and the knowledge, understanding and wisdom that comes with it. Invariably you gain an understanding of the process by which faith is applied. With this understanding you now know that the process is truth for *you*, and you have the evidence to prove it. You have acquired the ability to manage that which the Heavenly Father has given you, and hence, you become a good and faithful steward over that with which He entrusts to your keeping.

Wisdom is never far behind understanding, and understanding is never far from the knowledge gained through your experiences. Therefore, the *effective application* of knowledge *is* wisdom, and wisdom *is* power. But first comes knowledge, whether experienced, perceived or revealed, learning to understanding that which you *think* you know. Without understanding your experiences, is what you think you know truly knowledge? Without an understanding there is no knowledge that can be applied, and without knowledge there is no wisdom because it requires an understanding of what is known before it can be applied. And since there is no understanding then there can be no wisdom.

Please allow me to philosophize a moment! Wisdom is power because it is the truth, and it is the truth for you individually. There is particular truth that pertains only to you specifically, truth that applies only to your life, but there is also general truth that applies to everyone collectively; shared truth. It is true that the sun rises in the eastern sky and sets in the western sky. It is true that water is wet and fire is hot. You can know that fire is hot because someone has told you so. But do you understand that if you put your hand in that fire, you will get burned? Lacking an understanding you also lack wisdom, and because of your lack of wisdom you sense no threat, and you proceed to barbecue your hand. Through that experience comes wisdom. You understand now!

These are examples of shared truths. How you perceive that truth is a matter of your personal individuality, your inherent personality that adapts and responds to your environment and the people and things that you interact with. All the factors in *your* past and present life have influenced your being who *you* are at this point in time and space in your life.

Twenty people may witness an automobile accident, and there will invariably be twenty different versions of how the accident occurred. Simply because, individually, they have all seen the accident from different vantage points or physical locations than the nineteen other people; but many other factors determine how they perceive what happened, yet collectively they all witnessed the event.

The knowledge that you have applied, and especially the knowledge from which you have gained understanding and have experienced positive results, once reflected on, elicits the process or processes by which faith can continually be deployed to *practically* apply what you have come to understand, and that you have performed based on that knowledge you have obtained. The procedures of truth based faith that have proven to be effective in your life's experiences should be repeated, in much the same way as the yearly cultivating, planting, growing, and harvesting of crops or gardens is repeated.

At last, comes the season of the *feast!* It's time to enjoy the fruits of your labor. You get excited and become overjoyed as you move into your new abode. Afterward, you prepare a feast and invite friends, loved ones and most importantly, those who are less fortunate than you to come and partake of your bounty and blessings; the good fortune that GOD the Father has graced you with.

All who can, brings something to the feast, if no more than good humor. It's time for giving and sharing with each other in fellowship, expressing to them how your experience of faith has come to fruition and manifested prosperity for you; and everyone gives thanks to GOD, in season and out of season, for making manifest the object(s) of your faith, the fruit of your labor. It was well *earned!!!*

Now! Notice the joy that comes from experiencing a close and personal relationship with your Heavenly Father through Christ Jesus, Christ Michael the Master Creator Son of this universe. Experience the peace that overwhelms you, now having the absolute assurance that His love for you is unlike and unparalleled by anything or any other being in the Grand and Master Universes.

It is faith that makes a very personal relationship possible; not just having a superficial belief about who Christ Jesus was and is, and who His Father and ours always has been and will forever be, but seeking to really know them by always being *receptive* and listening for *their Word(s)* to come to you and then obeying them.

You will gradually come to understand and *practice* the *true religion* that Christ Jesus practiced as a *lifestyle* in human form; and being a one hundred percent human being He demonstrated that it is possible to know and to do GOD's Will.

If that is your true desire...*receive* Him and experience what it means to be in the kingdom of GOD the Father. Understand what it means to experience the power of being considered a son or daughter of GOD the Universal Father; for those who receive Him, to them He gave *power* to become sons of GOD.

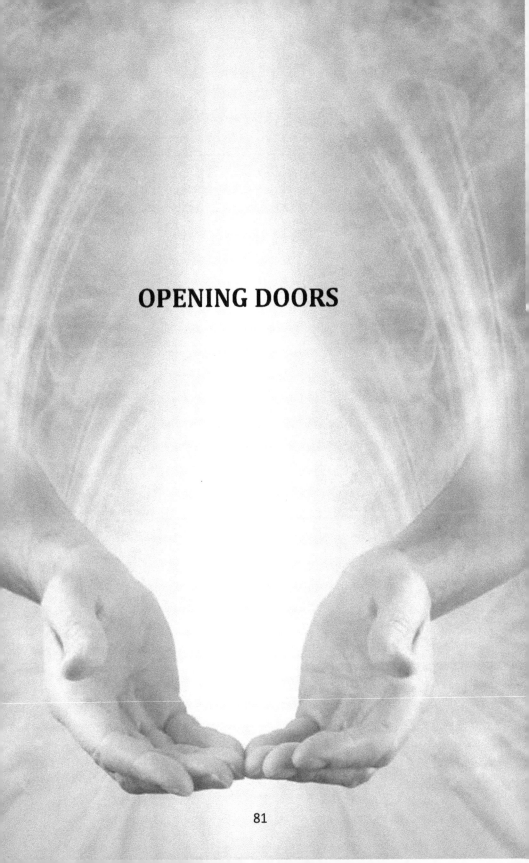

OPENING DOORS

Wˡhat is it that you need? What is it that you want or desire? It, whatever *it* is, is behind a closed door waiting to be opened by and with the key of faith, to afford you the opportunity to receive that thing, that *object* for which you seek.

In Scripture it is written that Christ Jesus said; "And I say unto you, Ask, and it shall be given you; seek, and you shall find; *knock*, and it shall be opened unto you. For everyone that asks receives; and he that seeks finds; and to him that *knocks* it shall be opened.

The things that Christ Jesus says should be taken very literally; meaning that He is saying exactly what He means. So, you should indeed and by action, **ask** the Father for what you need, want and desire. Why is that so difficult? It's a simple thing! Put aside the pride and humble yourself by first acknowledging Him. Say to Him; "Heavenly Father you are GOD the Creator! You are the First Source and Center of all that has ever been, all that exists now, and all that will ever be created."

Then ask Him for the *object* to which your faith is to be directed; the thing that you are exerting your energy and effort toward; the *physical* and *mental* activities you pursue in hopes that it should be the Father's Will to give, and that the object will become a spiritual, physical or material manifestation in your life experience.

If you have accepted and received by faith the ever accessible privilege of professing to be a son or daughter of GOD, then you are already in the kingdom of heaven; you are already counted among the sheep in the fold of the Creator Son of GOD, and He, Christ Jesus is the Good Shepherd tending His flock. He is the door through which the sheep in His fold enters and leaves. He is the door through which the abundant life opens up unto when accessed by faith and received in hope and expectation.

Of all the doors that may open up to us, the most important is the door through which is revealed the Source. This is even the Source of the faith that is required to inspire us to open the doors which contains the re-sources of that which we need or desire.

The Universal Father *is* that Source. He is the *First Source and Center!* Seek and you shall find what you're looking for…especially if what you seek is the truth. And again, you must physically and mentally exert energy!

Opening some of these doors may be difficult and time consuming, and some that looked easy and promising may not open at all. The *potential opportunity* that lies beyond is not meant for you. At least, it is not for you in the *season* which you are presently experiencing. Nevertheless, you should knock; *literally knock* on any door, so that the *potential opportunities* can open up and present themselves to you.

Consider this; you've been invited to a feast by some friends, you accept the invitation and on the day of the feast you go without eating in *anticipation* and *expectation* of partaking of the delights that you envision fills the tables. You go to the house and just stand outside *waiting* for someone to let you inside. All the window shades are closed and no one inside knows you are there. You, being outside have the ability to do the one thing necessary to gain entrance to the house, and let whoever is inside know that you are there, but you don't do it. That one thing is to knock. But if you absolutely and simply refuse to '*knock*' on the door you may never get inside to the feast…and this house has no doorbell or buzzer.

If you don't knock, how will *opportunity* know you are outside?

We have often heard the phrase, "door of opportunity," or perhaps, "window of opportunity." Both refer to, well…opportunity. The *door* of opportunity is the favorable conditions which exist, the favorable circumstances or situations that come when a door opens up and allows you to take advantage of the experience you receive from going through that door. *Sometimes* the experience leads directly to your prosperity, and sometimes to instruction and training,preparation to receive the object of your faith or your prosperity. The experience is always for your benefit and for your good.

The *window* of opportunity refers to the amount of *time* that exists in which you can take advantage of this particular opportunity, before it no longer produces the effect it may have yielded if recognized and pursued earlier, if it had been pursued in its season.

We are creatures of *time* and *space*, and there is nothing in our universe that is not relevant regarding time and that is not relative to space; in particular, the seasons of nature and the seasons of our lives. Whatever you do, wherever you go, it takes time.

Here is where patience is not only a virtue, but also a necessity! We will often…often have to wait. But there's no need to be idle just because we have to wait for certain conditions to occur. Do something that you think is relevant to your receiving the object of your faith.

Use those times as times of reflection to review the experiences that you've had during the course of your life. You should observe specific time frames in which your life courses have been similar as you regress farther into your past. You should realize that your life, your behavior and your mental processes the way you think and perceive life in general is affected by patterns of repeated routines and activities during certain periods, the recurring seasons in your life; routines and activities that are outside the realm of whatever habits or vices you may have acquired along the way.   But those things don't define you as a person nor as an individual. A person who as a son or daughter of the Father has a personal relationship with Him. It is your personality which originates in the Father and is distributed by the Eternal Son that defines you. It is your personal experiences that distinguish your ability to perceive the goodness of the Father as He opens doors *in their due season* and closes others, *making* you to lie down in green pastures so that He may restore your soul. During times of your restoration, you receive the training and the strength to endure what you must, so that you may receive the object of your faith.

Doors will open and they will close. Learn to recognize them and discern when they are open. The closed doors represent an opportunity in themselves. Just because they are closed for you at one point in time doesn't mean they are permanently closed for you. Be persistent! Keep knocking, keep trying to gain entrance, call out to the Father, "Father, I'm out here!"

Of course, He already knows that you're knocking, but how determined are you? How much do you need or desire the object you are requesting from Him? If you are sincere, He will respond to you, and in a way that you have no doubt that it is He who is responding directly and specifically to your request. Indeed, your sincerity is often shown *by* your persistence.

Nevertheless, notwithstanding your God-given common sense regarding how much time to afford a closed door to which you are attempting to gain entrance, give the Spirit of GOD within you His due diligence; allow Him to dictate when it's time to move on to pursue entrance to another door.

Whether or not an open door brings prosperity in some form spiritually, physically, mentally or materially depends much on the matter and manner in which your faith is applied and employed. But there are other factors involved, which include the environment in which you are operating, your knowledge and the ability to apply that knowledge (wisdom), and other factors too numerous to explore here. But walking through that door is an act of faith and actions will always produce knowledge through experience, and will elicit truth as *you* discern it to be based on *your* experience. Your experiences will produce fruit to the degree of your capacity to comprehend their meaning and how they relate to *your* life.

Have no fear! Walk through the doors that open up to you to experience what lies beyond. That is the biggest and most important condition that must be met as a means to apply your faith. How willing are you to trust the Father? How willing are you to believe that it is His Will that you receive the object of your faith that you have requested of Him?

How patient are you to wait until the opportunity does present itself, and how receptive are you to recognize, and then trust and believe the Spirit within you to reveal the opportunity when it appears? How aware will you be in perceiving the Spirit that beckons to you by the constant and persistent still small voice in your mind instructing you to do or not do a certain thing?

How willing are you to accept, believe and receive that which is being revealed to you as *your* truth; the way that is revealed for you as an individual, as a means to obtain, maintain and sustain that which the Heavenly Father prospers you with?

To state the obvious, not all opportunities present pleasant experiences. And in fact, some may be downright unpleasant. But there is always a lesson to be learned and experience to be had; and the degree to which you learn and apply the knowledge, skills and abilities that are naturally inherent within you and those that you obtain depends entirely on you.

RECOGNIZING AND RECEIVING THE OBJECT OF YOUR FAITH

People are material beings who have material and physical needs, and who have desires and wants. And neglected though they may be, people also have spiritual needs. The needs, desires and wants that are *spiritual* in nature consist in the obtaining of knowledge, understanding, and wisdom, but also of being endowed with the discernment of truth and the Fruit of the Spirit.

Physical needs and desires are those things that relate to health and well being; things like the healing of sickness and disease, or food and other things necessary to maintain, sustain and improve one's life and health. But as long as hatred, greed and lust persists in this world there will always be material needs and wants that require money to obtain them. Most material things fall into one of these categories; necessities, wants or the desires of your heart.

Accordingly, materially minded people seem to have an inherent instinct to seek the biggest, the best and the most expensive things possible as the object of their desire. They seem to think that because they are expecting to receive what they have prayed for or requested from the Father, the Source, the Giver and the Supplier of what is asked, then what they are to receive is going to be some grand material object, or some magnificent revelation and they expect it to appear suddenly miraculously. As the result, the object of their desire, the thing for which they have asked is often not received because of their totally selfish and exaggerated needs or expectations. They expect something other than what the Heavenly Father has for them.

How often does a person ask GOD for something in faith, and they do the things that are required of them in order to receive the object of their faith, yet the self serving object of their misplaced faith eludes them because they refuse to accept that which the Father has given them? Instead, they continue to pursue what *they* want rather than what the Father has already given and made available to them. What GOD the First Source and Center gives you, He is infinitely able to sustain you with while having it. He provides the means that allows us to maintain and sustain what He gives to His children.

THE KEYS TO PROSPERITY MANIFESTATION

What He gives us is always better, though it may not seem so at the time. He is our Heavenly Father and He knows what is best for us, even more so than good parents knows what is best for their child.

This is not to imply that you shouldn't attempt to obtain the biggest and the best, because you may have attained the spiritual station in life where upon receiving that biggest and best, you will be grateful for it and use it to your benefit and the benefit of others. You may already have obtained the skills or knowledge that is required to maintain it and be a worthy steward of whatever your faith object may be. It makes little or no practical sense, nor good common sense to qualify for an expensive house or car and you get it, but then not be able to pay the mortgage or note without having to sacrifice some other basic need like food, or to pay utility bills and buy fuel for your car. Yet this is often the case and the result is usually a perpetual state of worry, stress and depression, not to mention probable bankruptcy or repossession.

There is much expressed in scripture in regard to *giving*. And that is as it should be because the *essence* of love is *giving* and *forgiving*. "For GOD so *loved* the world, that He '*gave*' His begotten Son, that whosoever believes in Him should not perish, but have everlasting life."

But just as much emphasis is placed on '*receiving*' as there is on giving. And again, this is as it should be. It is written that Christ Jesus said, "Ask and it shall be given you."

In the days when Christ Jesus lived among men, the Chief Priests and religious leaders exploited fearful, unlearned and ignorant people, appealing to their guilty conscious' in order to obtain wealth or to achieve some other self-serving motive. And since then, nothing has changed. Foolish people still succumb to religious leaders who employ a few scriptures in the Bible to relieve unwary individuals of their much-needed money, money they need to fulfill even their most basic needs. When will people realize that scriptures, and indeed, the whole Bible was written as a record and history of just one group of people who occupy this world? And that it was not meant to be a standard that every human being is to live by.

Obviously, little emphasis is placed on *receiving* in institutionalized houses of worship (churches). Rather, the emphasis there is placed on giving...to them. Consider this; if people actually gave their money *and time* in support of the people whom they see in their everyday pursuits that are in need, the church's mission would be much easier to accomplish. Together with spiritual teaching, the church would in fact *be* accomplishing its' true purpose. Those who are the church, those of the household of faith would be performing 'service' to their fellow human beings, and in doing so would be portraying the type of love expected of the children of GOD. They would be exhibiting brotherhood and sisterhood and actually become inhabitants of the kingdom of GOD the Father. This is the manner in which we express our love to the Paradise Father, GOD the Sevenfold.

The true church's mission, which is to convey the gospel of the Kingdom of heaven to everyone, would be more readily accepted as genuine and real, when the material things that we have been blessed with are shared with those in need.

It is a fact of life that there will always be those who are in need. Christ Jesus, being the Creator, acknowledges as much; but material prosperity is a matter of chance and choice sometimes, and it is always the result of GOD's Will or what He allows.

The manner in which you *receive* as a matter of *choice*, comes by your choosing to prepare yourself; to educate yourself so that you may have a better *chance* amid the population of those who are also seeking to obtain prosperity, and from the same secular resource from which you are seeking it. Earthly resources are limited in relation to the world's population, but there are no limits when prosperity is sought from the Source...GOD the Father.

Choice is your willful act; the work that you exert or the *deeds* that you choose to perform which you believe or you hope will result in your obtaining prosperity. These things may come through the natural course of your secular activities.

You go to school and college, self educate or otherwise get an education, and then you apply for a job and you get it. Afterward, you work diligently and over time you acquire or obtain a semblance of prosperity.

Chance is that phenomenon that enables you to be in the right place at the right time for you to receive the elements leading to the prosperity that you seek. It is neither chance nor choice that determines who will be born into a wealthy family or conversely into an impoverished one, or somewhere in between.

The Heavenly Father predestines events to happen, allowing them to run their natural course. You were predestined to be who you are where you are. We as human beings make our own choices, given the social environment in which we are born, choices which increase or decrease the chances of being prosperous.

Chance also to some degree, determines all that befalls us in life; to some degree because spiritual, natural and physical laws and the *choices* we make in consonance with these laws determines the rest, and these laws always prevail except where GOD's Will and your faith intervenes.

His Will is the ever enduring and inevitable fulfillment of His purpose and plan for you and all of His created beings in all the universes of time, space and eternity. His Will *can* overcome and overpower your will, but that would defeat His purpose of allowing His created beings to have free will. It is not His way to force or impose His Will upon anyone. He desires that His children willingly acknowledge Him as their Father by their own volition. Still, He allows you to decide within yourself to follow your own path or the path that He has predestined for you. This predestined path is revealed as you learn to heed the leading of His Spirit within you, and as you learn to recognize the guidance and directions of the ministering Spirits and Beings assigned to you, and as you adjust your actions in response to their prompting.

His path leads you on a quest that persistently seeks truth, beauty and goodness. While on the quest, you will invariably be seeking His kingdom, for you will realize that GOD and His righteousness are the same. And when you enter the Kingdom of GOD, therein, you will discover the way for you to *receive by faith*, the things that he has already prepared for you to receive. Your Heavenly Father has already given you many things. However, you must *receive* these things by faith, continually applying all of the components of genuine faith that are necessary to make manifest *all these things* and obtain lasting prosperity.

When you receive things by faith, by applying faith's principles, the experience is enhanced and thoroughly gratifying when you know that you have accessed the realm of true spiritual reality the kingdom of heaven to bring your faith object to manifestation.

CONTRAST BETWEEN RELIGION
AND
SPIRITUALITY

The practices of traditional religion encompass the masses of people, attempting to condition them into conforming to standardized, denominational and institutional beliefs, principles and doctrines; much of which, because of misrepresentation and incorrect interpretation of scripture, impose a heavy burden on people to be borne. *Bondage* by any other name is still bondage, just in another form. Many are totally unaware that they are under bondage, and if they did perhaps it would make little if any difference to them, for they are in their comfort zone. Still, there may be those who would like to be made aware that this type of bondage that is so prevalent and overbearing, that its effects leave the person under very much the same kind of bondage spiritually, as does physical bondage. This is a subtle bondage that renders efforts to apply faith fruitless; as those efforts have been taught and believed, and leaves many prayers and supplications unmanifested; leaving needs and desires unfulfilled and prosperity unattained.

So, it becomes necessary to differentiate between the true religion and institutional religion, for in knowing the difference, you can all the better choose which form you will practice. Will you choose the true religion which welcomes you into the kingdom of GOD the Father and increases your knowledge, understanding and faith in spiritual reality, and that increases the potentials for your faith objects to manifest as you discover your station as a son or daughter of GOD? Or will you continue to choose institutional religion with its spiritual growth and faith limiting bonds of ceremonies, rituals and traditions?

"Paganized and socialized Christianity stands in need of new contact with the Uncompromised teachings of Jesus; it languishes for lack of a new vision of the Master's life on earth. A new and fuller revelation of the religion of Jesus is destined to conquer an empire of materialistic secularism and to overthrow a world sway of mechanistic naturalism. Urantia (earth) is now quivering on the very brink of one of its most amazing and enthralling epochs of social readjustment, moral quickening, and spiritual enlightenment."

Institutional religion has become a hard taskmaster, requiring its servants to produce something that cannot come to fruition simply because inappropriate and ineffective tools are being given and used for the tasks at hand. Institutional religion requires your loyalty to denominational doctrine and monotonous ceremony rather than your diligence in search of an understanding of the revealed knowledge of the Kingdom of Heaven and your devotion to *"truth."* It maintains its strength and control through misinformation and half or part truths, occasionally distracting its subjects from their main objective...their pursuit of money; and it leaves the truth seekers' hunger unfulfilled.

The *"true religion"* encourages giving, but the giving of yourself in service. Not in redundant and fruitless ceremonies and rituals which gives lip-service as worship of GOD the Father; but rather, through individual devotion and worship that focuses on giving honor and praise to our Heavenly Father on a personal and private level. It promotes the giving of genuine love; which, as Christ Jesus showed, is not beyond our ability to give.

Some people seem to think that our Heavenly Father requires his children to give beyond their means, even borrowing money to give to a church for some function or another; or even borrowing money to help someone when doing so leaves the borrower or giver in a state of want. These people think that this proves that they love and serve others. While their unwise actions may ease the deluded person's conscious and perhaps bring comfort to someone in need, it hardly proves that they are expressing love, and it certainly is not required by the Father to give beyond your means at the time. Yet this too is your choice.

Once the truth is revealed, once the blinders are lifted from the eyes of those who seek to discover the Master's religion, the religion 'of ' Christ Jesus, which was a life of seeking to know and then, doing the will of His Father, then you will come to realize the futility in continuing in a quasi-faith religion.

Differentiation must be made between being spiritual and being religious because the two however related are inherently different. Religion, *institutional religion* as it is commonly practiced may be a means, a vehicle if you will, by which *knowledge* of the Father, Son and Spirit is obtained, but that's as far as it will take you. It is limited in function and in bringing forth effective results, and it is only one narrow avenue to discovering the true religion.

There are different sources from which truth and knowledge regarding the Paradise Trinity and all the other beings of the Heavenly hosts can be found. It is just a matter of seeking them, searching for truths and once finding them, coming to your own conclusions and interpretations about what is meant.

What? Do you think that the Father only speaks through preachers and teachers? Do you think that your Father can't speak to you like He speaks to those who call themselves ministers and preachers, the clergy? The Heavenly Father speaks to 'all' who diligently and sincerely seek Him. He wants you to know Him, but humans can only receive so much knowledge about Him at any given time, and it is the Mystery Monitor, the Spirit of the Father within you that reveals Him as you are able to receive His enlightening and liberating revelations.

"True religion the religion of revelation. The revelation of supernatural values, a partial insight into eternal realities, a glimpse of the goodness and beauty of the infinite character of the Father in heaven the religion of the spirit as demonstrated in human experience."

Institutional religion can only take you so far because mankind, no matter how bright, intelligent or smart we are can only know so much. The human capacity for knowledge is finite. Our brain has inherent limitations, but despite its inherent limitations, our capacity to receive truth can be expanded by the Spirit of GOD that dwell within us...by your spirit.

All knowledge, understanding, wisdom, and everything else in fact and in truth comes from GOD the Father; and wisdom finds expression through GOD the Eternal Son, who imparts to all of His created beings the real WORD of GOD personally and individually according to our capacity to understand. Along with GOD the Infinite Spirit, the Paradise Trinity possesses all knowledge, understanding and wisdom. Their capacity to know and do anything is without limits and boundaries except those that they impose upon themselves.

Institutional religion can only generate a spark of curiosity about things you may peruse or study in Biblical scripture as it is expressed and explained, and as it is understood by the listener, you the *seeker*. It should ignite within you a growing desire to know more about Them, the Paradise Trinity. It should help motivate you to discover just what Their relationship to you and with you *is*, and what a personal relationship with them truly means for you.

True religion is the teacher of the students of spirituality, and students of spirituality are those who seek the kingdom of GOD; knowing with all assurance that when once we enter, therein, all these things shall be added unto us. For all things spiritual comes to us through the Word of GOD, GOD the Eternal Son, and is made manifest in us by the Spirit of GOD that dwell within us. Just as words express how we feel, how they express our emotions and our actions and intentions, GOD the Eternal Son *and* Christ Jesus the incarnate person of Christ Michael is the expression of GOD's Love and also the expression of His Will for *our* life and the lives of all beings of His creations. The Word of GOD and I don't mean the Bible; I mean GOD the Eternal Son inspires and encourages the deeper questions about eternal and spiritual matters.

A very wise person has said, "The questioning of ecclesiastical scripture is the beginning of wisdom." The true religion causes us to ponder questions about the universe and all that exists herein. We begin to have questions about our planet, its history and our own creation. It engenders the desire to know more of our own spirituality, our relationship with GOD our Father. And when traditional institutional religion does not know the answers, the truth, then we must *seek it* where it can be found. But we must *seek it!* And *seek* it some more! us...personally; with our own eyes and ears and within our capacity to understand. The truth will resonate within our heart. The truth that we discern is the truth as GOD the Father would have us know and experience it now. For now, *this* moment is all we ever really have.

Truth gravitates to truth. And the seeker of truth will find it. And when you find it, you will know it as the truth, because along with the truth comes its discernment. The Spirit of Truth has already been poured out on '*all*' flesh so that when the truth that you seek is discovered, the spirit within you affirms it to be truth by some means of confirmation; but mostly by an increase in faith, causing unwavering belief and confidence that we have in fact discovered the *truth* concerning the matter of our spiritual quest.

Institutional religion tends to employ the emotion of fear very effectively to bind the conscious minds of its adherents; causing them to see the Heavenly Father as a vengeful and wrathful

GOD, who will reward you if you do what is written in scripture or punish you if you don't. These methods are employed to coerce unwary, fearfully superstitious and gullible people into submission. They surrender their own will, and blindly fulfill the agendas of the leaders of these institutions, and their agendas are seldom commensurate with the Heavenly Father's Will.

Fear and guilt sufficiently and continuously limits spiritual insight and hinders spiritual growth and progress. These faith nullifying traits serves to distort spiritual reality and truth. Practicing this kind of religion interferes with the free will process of all human beings that have will; using superstitious fear and guilt to perpetuate exact compliance to denominational religious or church doctrine and to conform to their doctrine; hence exercising a form of religious control over the minds of their congregants.

The practice of this kind of religion limits and retards faith to the point of hopeless redundancy and futile efforts to grow spiritually. It disguises itself as a warm and intense *emotional* experience enabled by the talented, eloquent and stimulating rhetoric and showmanship of the preacher or person of the clergy. These congregants little realize that they are only succumbing and responding to that stimulus, and all the while being conditioned to receive and believe only the ministers' faith limiting interpretation of Scripture; the preacher's interpretations being the perpetuation, propagation and reflection of some larger governing body of institutional religion over that denomination. These governing bodies outline and instructs prospective preachers on how scripture is to be expressed, and really, how they are to condition their congregations, lulling them into a passive and conforming state of mind.

Religious experiences like those often displayed in churches, however warm and fuzzy they may be, does not present accurate portrayals of the Heavenly Father nor His Son and their Will and purpose for *your* life. Half truths and non truths do not by faith bring to fruition the manifestation of the object(s) for which you pray, meditate and submit your supplications; they do not afford you the personal spiritual experiences that a liberated mind allows.

The true religion reveals GOD the Father who has unconditional Love for all of His created beings. For those who genuinely seek Him, to all who sincerely seek the true religion of Christ; those who practice applying faith principles and endeavor to apply the truths that personal life experiences have taught, you shall truly be *born again*. You will enjoy the manifestation of your faith objects as they become genuine *spiritual* experiences in a manner that redirects your attitudes and behaviors. There is no greater mortal experience than the confirmation that GOD is your Father and you are His child. True religion releases the kind of active and interactive faith that, in time, actually brings the *object* to which your *faith* is *directed* into existence and into your personal experience.

The object was *pre-existent* before even the thought of the object enters your mind. Only then can faith be applied; then the *potential* object that you begin to contemplate can be made manifest, can become *actual*. It is within your capabilities to *direct your faith* toward many things. But not all at once! Pursue a little at a time. Oh, it's not because the Father can't handle all the requests for your needs, but rather, it's because *you* may not be able to devote the attention to detail when you are performing the actions and works required to bring the objects into your material, physical or spiritual reality.

Having too many objects to which your faith is directed may distract you from *recognizing* that another object is in readiness to be made manifest into your material reality, and it could go unclaimed because you failed to receive it. Being so busy trying to do the work required for all your other faith objects, you did not take the necessary actions required for each specific object to come into your possession…this is often the case. Even the above average human among us can only do so much.

Nevertheless, there are other reasons why it *seems* that prayers and supplications do not come to fruition or seem to go unanswered. Simply because we don't visibly, materially or physically receive the object of faith in what may be consider a reasonable time or even in this life time, one may presume that their prayer has gone unanswered or neglected and give up. Be assured, it has not gone neglected. Though you may not receive the objects or answers to your prayers in this mortal life, you shall indeed receive them in a life after this very short one.

We often don't even know what we need or want. The circumstances and situations in our life may be so overwhelming that we can barely think, much less verbally or mentally express what we need. In these times the Spirit Fragment of the Father that He has endowed us with, our spirit, His spirit that dwells within our minds makes intercession for us. It may take time to really determine our need. Because It (the indwelling Thought Adjuster, the Mystery Monitor) must determine what we are actually expressing, and what He, the Spirit knows that we actually need and what is best for us. Our GOD Fragment knowing the Father's Will, then proceeds to coordinate with the Seraphic hosts and other ministering spirits to bring about the conditions that in time brings your petitions to fruition in accordance with His Will.

In essence, the true religion is the religion '*of*' Christ Jesus, the religion that He practiced, lived and taught, rather than the pseudo religion '*about*' Him. It is the religion 'of' Christ Jesus that produces the power to become sons and daughters of GOD the Father; and it is in the seeking to always do the Father's Will, and in the rendering of service to our fellow brothers and sisters, and in living our life by faith that the true religion is expressed.

LIVING YOUR LIFE
BY FAITH

Spirituality pertains to all things in the spiritual realm, things that are unseen. And it requires faith for mortal beings in this physical and material realm of reality the realm in which we currently exist to pierce the veil between the two realms. It requires that we continually apply the faith apportioned to us by wholeheartedly believing and trusting in the spiritual reality, that GOD is our Heavenly Father and that we are His children. Perceive the spiritual reality even more than you sense the physical and material reality.

Piercing the veil into spiritual reality requires that you yield your will to the Will of the Father, and begin the actual *living* of the Spirit led life; and part of living a Spirit led life is in the discovering of how personally and materially liberating it is. Your attitude, your behavior and your actions, now becomes the responsibility of the Holy Spirit, the ministering spirits and your GOD Fragment within. You can have the utmost confidence and assurance that GOD the Father oversees everything that pertains to you, His child.

All too often people put on an air of piety, and in front of others they may exhibit a self righteous and pious behavior by sheer will power. Those seemingly pious people are sometimes critical of those who cannot portray as strong a will to even temporarily demonstrate the pious person's degree of self-denial or restraint.

But once you begin to apply and exercise your faith, and understanding your seasons, you come to realize true spirituality. It begins to happen when you acknowledge, accept and receive your son-ship or daughter ship into the kingdom of GOD. You will over time- begin to naturally and genuinely exhibit the Fruit of the Spirit.

Why do people so often concern themselves with what others think about them? They allow others to dictate to them how to live their lives. Far too many churchgoers think that because a person doesn't attend church regularly, or attend at all, that that person is doomed to hell (as if there was such a place...). Not only has this critical person *judged* the non churchgoer, but they would also sentence them to an eternity of hell fire and brimstone.

You allow people to put you on guilt trips because you feel somewhat inadequate and way too self conscious and insecure. And like a lion can sense weakness in its prey, your vulnerability is exposed; because you have little or no confidence and trust in your own power or the power of your Heavenly Father's ability to lead you in the way that *He* has purposed for your life.

The Father doesn't need an intermediary to speak to you, He can and does communicate directly with you, both consciously and subconsciously. The Father doesn't need someone else telling you their interpretations of spiritual truth and reality, or telling you how you should live your life. GOD the Father can and does tell you personally through His Fragment the Thought Adjuster, His Spirit that indwells you.

He could coerce or force us to live our life the way He desires, but He leaves those choices up to us. Rather, He directs and guides us all along the journey of our progression to perfection and allows us to hear and follow His guidance. This is truly GOD's Word and He speaks it directly to you, specifically for you.

When people advise you on any matter, they are giving you advice based upon their experiences, and sometimes based solely on their opinion. Their advice to you may be something they wouldn't even consider doing themselves, but they take pleasure in advising you to do it. These people revel in the knowledge that you have given them power over your life.

Your Heavenly Father desires that *you* should live your own life, and not let others live their life through you, and not allow others to experiment with your life; seeing how you will fare in a given situation. And if something unpleasant perchance befalls you...well, it's not them! If your Heavenly Father wanted them to have your life and your experiences, He would have given your life to them. And He would have given their life to you or someone else. You do have a life... don't you?

GOD our Heavenly Father has given us a personality, and He gave us a body in which to accommodate the lifestyle that we choose to live; a body capable of fulfilling His purpose for our life. It is a life relative to our environment and our ability to learn from it and adapt to it in a manner that helps us survive, prosper and progress. The things that we learn often act as a deterrent, guarding against harmful things. But the things we learn also provide motivation for us to apply the principles of universal truths that we have learned through our life's experiences, truths that when applied will benefit us and our fellow brothers and sisters. Even when faith principles that are based in truth are unwittingly or unknowingly applied *correctly*, such applied faith still makes manifest the object hoped for. The *process* still works.

As you discover your new found liberty, know that the more you seek to do the Will of the Father with sincere effort and with love, the more courageous you become and the more assertive you will be in quelling the unneeded advice and guidance of others. Though well intentioned and sometimes good advice is given, they can only give you the benefit of their experience, in perhaps a similar situation, but not in *your* situation.

We are to contemplate and perhaps heed wise advice and counsel, but ultimately the decisions about our life are ours to make, with due consideration and the understanding that our life is our responsibility...not theirs! Likewise, in your advising, counseling, consoling and assuring others, do realize the same about the life of your fellow human being in their time of distress or discomfort. Earnest and honest efforts which are displayed through service for our earthly companions, our brothers and sisters, is indeed the Father's Will for all of His being's possessing personality.

You can live a life of morality and righteousness in accordance with your perception and understanding of what a moral and righteous life entails; even though your belief systems may not be synonymous with those of the religious mainstream. You can still live a life based upon the true religion of Christ Jesus.

His religion is one based on knowing the fallibility of humans; their fears, their beliefs, their inclinations as dictated by their natural instincts and environments. The religion of Jesus allows you to live your life as you choose to live it. Free from the opinions of the so called righteous, and free from conformity to doctrines that incorporates ritualistic and ceremonial practices that delimits the expression of your personal spiritual individuality. But there are two things in particular that distinguishes the religion *'of'* Jesus from the religions of men and the religion *'about'* Jesus.

First and foremost, the religion of Christ always, in every situation He sought to know and to do the Heavenly Father's Will. Secondly His religion frees us from any and all fear and guilt associated with the weaknesses and vices that are common to mankind on this sphere which many denounce as sin.

In regard to living your own life, the Universal Father instead encourages you to acknowledge, accept and receive Him as your GOD, your Father in Paradise, the Creator of all that is, was and all that will ever be in time, space and eternity. He desires to impart to you the power you will receive when you sincerely believe and acknowledge that you are a son or daughter of your Heavenly Father.

When once you determine to accept all human beings as children of GOD your Father, you must also determine to accept them as they are, imperfect...just as you are, just as we all are. But recognize that the same potential that you have to progress and eventually become perfect, they also have the potential to attain perfection.

It doesn't matter that some of your brothers and sisters have defects; physical and or mental aberrations, not to mention undesirable attitudes and behaviors. Some people regularly display almost intolerable behavior as part of their undeveloped spiritual personality; you may sometimes be repulsed by their attitudes, their attributes and even their physical appearances. But they are your brothers and sisters nonetheless.

But when you find aberrations or defective attitudes and behaviors in one of your fellow human beings to be morally unconscionable and reprehensible, the Spirit of GOD who dwells within you will assert Himself and bring to your awareness, the fact that you too have defects and faults that others may feel the same way about. How would you like for them to treat you?

We are one huge family, the family of the human races of this planet, the family of GOD, citizens of the universe and true religious spirituality; and living your life by faith perpetuates and propagates unity - though not conformity to any religious rituals of communal social gatherings. For although many people may by consensus agree on an issue, doctrine or principle, that does not make them true nor does it make the subject matter of the consensus GOD's Will and purpose.

True Living by faith operates and acts upon the principle of *"loving the Lord our GOD with all our heart, with all our mind, and with all our strength;"* this is the first commandment, and you can be certain that this is the Heavenly Father's Will...for everybody! But it also facilitates service and love for our fellow human beings, encouraging us to "do unto others as we would have them do unto us," which is to "love our neighbor as we love ourselves."

We are personally endowed with a Spirit Fragment of GOD the Universal Father. It is the Spirit of GOD that dwells within us...our spirit. If you so desire and you ask for the Spirit's Fruit, you will receive it, and you will be able to accept all people as your brother or sister of humanity and within, you will have genuine and unpretentious love for them. Nobody said it would be easy...it's not! But it's necessary and often rewarding to make the effort.

Notwithstanding, love does necessitate an attempt to lovingly correct morally defective behavior in one of your brothers or sisters as you are led to do so. But be sure that it is the Spirit of GOD that's leading you to correct or rebuke them and not your own self-righteous ego; bearing in mind your own deficiencies. Remove the beam that's in your own eye and then you can see more clearly to remove the mote in someone else's eye.

And be cautious not to judge someone who is presumed to be morally defective as determined by the morality standards of man, for their perception is distorted by their own unacknowledged and unrepentant immoral acts; acts which they often refuse to acknowledge in themselves *as* being immoral. The standards that you employ in judging others are the same standards by which the Ancients of Days will judge you after your resurrection on the first mansion world, should you choose to survive. So…can you measure up to your own moral standards?

We are all animals and subject to the natural basic animal instincts that other animals have; the natural instincts for survival and procreation. Our Heavenly Father understands this and supplies an abundance of 'grace' and 'mercy,' pouring them into the mix to more than compensate for our animal desires…*He forgives*! If indeed forgiveness is required. Still, the natural course of life dictates that justice and righteousness prevails. Hence, what you sow, you will reap in time. And the return, the harvest that you reap is often more than you sowed, be they good seeds or undesirable seeds.

Understand the kind of unconditional love that our Heavenly Father has for us in so much that He does allow corrective measures in the form of trials, tribulations and troubles to befall us, but these things are not some form of punishment. They are things that are common to human kind as we traverse this uncertain maze of life. They are often the efforts of celestial beings of the Heavenly host trying to bring you to a more spiritual state or to the behavior that you are to portray as a child of GOD; and the more true GOD like behavior we possess will make the faith that we deploy fruitful. Love allows us to humbly acknowledge and accept correction from our fellow human beings and chastening by the Father; the subduing and restraining of good things by the Father in heaven when undesirable behavior is practiced by you.

We all share this sphere, this planet which *we* call earth (Urantia). Life on this planet with all of our adventures and misadventures, with all of our fortunes and misfortunes, our trials and tribulations, and with all of our joys and sorrows, places all of us on equal footing. No matter your status or station in life; be you rich or poor, of one race or another, intellectually gifted or intellectually deficient, religious or otherwise, we all have this physical, material and spiritual gauntlet to accept or to throw down. Life is a challenge, and once we can finally realize that we need each other and begin to treat one another as we would like to be treated, the sooner humanity will come to be what our Heavenly Father intends for us to be…His truly loving sons and daughters of faith!

Living your life by faith consists of being patient and believing and trusting; trusting the Father completely; believing that His love for His created beings dictates what He does in regard to us, which is to love us and take care of us…*as He* sees fit and *when* He sees fit! The Father's will does engender your actions whether you are aware and conscience of them or not. It is the Father's Will that you have choices, and that you depend on and trust in His Fatherly guidance and revelations so you can make choices that benefit yourself and others; the choices that will lead you right to Him.

Sometimes people do things and they have no idea why they would have done such a thing. Innocent though their action may be, that is, if no one is in any way harmed or put in dangers path, that action may perchance be in accordance with GOD's Will, an action that they spontaneously performed. But as you recognize and obey the call -as revealed by the Spirit of GOD the Father within you to mobilization, and you do so, you move ever closer to your prosperity and to fulfilling His Will and purpose for your life.

To fully and wholeheartedly acknowledge, accept, believe and *act* on the truth that "*All things* work together for good to them that love GOD, to them who are the called according to His purpose," is to *act* and *live* by faith. How so? Except for the commandments that Jesus, the Son of GOD expressed as being the Will of the Father, we can't always in this life be entirely certain about just what His Will is for people as individuals. It is only *after* the manifestation of an object that through an act of faith for which you have asked becomes manifest that the assurance, from that spiritual experience elicits the knowledge that it was indeed His Will that you receive the object, or that you attain to another level of *spiritual experience*.

Although the situation or circumstance that you find yourself in may not be at all good or pleasant, the end result will be to *your* benefit and for *your* good...as GOD the *Father* determines your good. What *you consider* to be for your good and what the Father *knows* is for your good, may not be the same.

The Paradise Father is viewing your good from an eternal and infinite perspective, and you are viewing it from yours, a carnal and material point of view depending upon your station in life. Whether that station is one of mediocre means, endeavoring to survive one day at a time, or one of the grand and grandiose proclivities of the wealthy, having everything at one's disposal; or whether your station is somewhere in between, you will be forever grateful and thoroughly satisfied with the end results in whatever station in life you may find yourself at any particular point in time. By faith you can always attain to another level, if it is the Father's Will. His version of what is for your good is always perpetually better!

Directing your faith is accomplished through meditation, prayer and supplications to the Father; praying in the name of the Master Creator Son of this Universe, the incarnate person of Christ Jesus, and praying as He taught His apostles and disciples to pray; acknowledging and praising the Father for who He is, thanking Him in advance for the requested desire. We must always be very specific and to the point when we by faith make a petition to our Father!

You have perhaps heard the saying: "Be careful what you pray for, you just might get it!" Don't take that saying for granted! The *way* that your prayers are answered is often unpredictable. The means by which prayers are answered often brings unintended and unwanted circumstances in the *process* of their manifestation and may come in a form that is neither desired nor recognized as being a condition or your preparation as the means to your prayer being answered. But regardless of the form, whenever it comes to fruition it will be for your good.

There is a lesson to be learned during the process of manifesting the object to which you have directed your faith. Reflect on what that lesson might be and once you are enlightened, apply that knowledge; for the *application* of knowledge is wisdom.

Take time daily to simply sit relaxed and meditate. Clear your mind of any and everything and try to find that inner space where you are alone and still. Then when you are alone and still, visualize the object of your faith, projecting it, *directing it* in silence to GOD the Universal Father, the First Source and Center.

Thoughts will naturally invade your mind but with practice, you will be able to better focus on your faith object and in due time whether short or long in duration the method, the process by which you are to obtain that object is revealed and a fire ignites within you motivating you to act. You become in tune with the mind of Christ; the Spirit of Truth.

Continue *hoping*, and by the actions that you take, the *work* that you do that is directly *related to your receiving of the object* from the Father, if it is His Will, it will be made manifest to you. You will receive it either on this world or over the course of time on one of the many mansion worlds which you will traverse in your ascension to Paradise and your progression to spiritual GOD like perfection.

You will learn the prodding, the prompting, and the nudging of the Seraphic Guardians of Destiny (your guardian angels) as they manipulate environments in their attempts to guide you in knowing and doing the Father's Will. You will discern the teaching and comforting of the Holy Spirit in times of disappointment and sorrow as well as the joy and contentment with His assurance that you are His son or daughter, a child of the eternal and infinite GOD. You will be enlightened by your indwelling Thought Adjuster who gently and sometimes, not so gently goes into action within your mind and conscious until you are aware of and attentive to His revelation that is specifically for you.

Through the course of your *spiritual experiences,* you receive revelations of knowledge, instructing you in just what work it is that you should be doing and the indwelling GOD Fragment leads you to it and supports you through it. The Spirit prepares you to receive that which in time will be made manifest...the object of your faith.

Whatever the subject matter of your query is, or whatever the object of your faith is, the work to be done is the thing that the Thought Adjuster prompts you to do and the Holy Spirit enlightens and gives assurance to you in the doing. That process will be first and foremost in your mind until you do it, and the Spirit of Truth gives you conformation for He is the Comforter and the Mighty Councilor. Your mind is the domicile of the Spirit of GOD dwelling within you. You won't be able to rest or have peace of mind until you do what is being required of you to do...the work, or until you acknowledge and accept the truth that you were seeking as the truth of your request, whether it be a personal, spiritual, social or of some other issue.

Don't quench the Spirit, do what your conscience is admonishing you to do, or quit doing what it is admonishing you not to do. There will be times when you are not certain that it is your indwelling GOD Fragment guiding you. Test the Spirit! If the work continues to relentlessly invade your thoughts, but at the same time being undemanding, this is the manner of workings by your Thought Adjuster. You can be sure that if it is the Spirit of GOD guiding you that He won't prompt you to do anything against the *expressed* laws and Will of GOD the Father and GOD the Son. The Spirit will not prompt you to do anything that will cause harm to you or your fellow human beings...your brothers and sisters! Do it, or stop doing it, as you are prompted.

You should not be overly concerned about any perceived consequences that you may encounter because of your actions. You may not know in this life what part your actions played in bringing about the end result, the manifestation of the object of your faith. But just knowing that your efforts certainly had something to do with your faith object coming to fruition, and that at least that much of faith does work, should serve to give you assurance that the whole process works.

Now, because you have displayed faith, because you have expressed trust in the Father and believe in Him, you believe that His Will is to give you the object you hope for, in due time, and in due season whatever the object that your faith has been directed toward, it will be made known, becoming the evidence of your faith. It will materialize and become a part of your physical, material and spiritual experience. *You* must believe *that* as well…wholeheartedly so. Your faith object will become the proof, the *evidence* that it came to fruition *by faith*.

This is a faith that does not *need* the manifestation of material objects to acknowledge and accept that our Universal Father is the *First Source and Center* of *all things*; but after you have gone through the process of *practically applying* faith, and you acknowledge it as such, the manifestation of the object of your faith incites rejoicing in your heart, and your faith is increased and strengthened when the physical materialization of the object is realized, when *potential* becomes *actual*.

You are thrilled beyond your capacity to contain your spiritual experience within and you can't help but share your experience with someone else. Then your hunger and thirst for more revelations of truth increases; that truth, which when applied produced the *evidence* of your faith, it grows stronger. And as each object to which you have *directed your faith* becomes manifest and realized, and as the answer to any spiritual quandary is revealed, and as your perplexing or trying situation is resolved, you truly learn to trust GOD the Heavenly Father, *as* your Father who only wants the best for His faith sons and daughters. Now you begin having complete assurance and confidence that, "He will supply all our needs according to His riches in glory."

True religion encourages you to be *patient*, to wait for both the revealing of truth, and for the manifesting of the object of your faith. There is a tried-and-true process which begins your spiritual growth while you are here on earth, and continues after this mortal life ends, until your spiritual progress earns you the status of being 'perfect, and that only happens when you enter Paradise and become like GOD the Universal Father.

There are celestial beings and ministering spirits of the Master Creator Son and His Associate Spirit, the Creative Mother Spirit, the Divine Minister His Consort that assists in your spiritual development and progress. It takes time for your preparation and for conditions to exist through the natural course of events in *your* life that will bring forth the *evidence*, the *substance*, the objects of your faith into your material existence.

Having patience is absolutely essential to the process of applying faith. It is *part of* the process. It takes time for you to be prepared to receive those objects. You must go through some things! You will have issues that try you in every way imaginable, but this is no test that the Heavenly Father subjects you to as a means to determine how you will react in a given situation and under certain conditions...He already knows! They are the means by which, like the raw material that makes iron or steel goes through a process of separating impure materials that will corrupt it, and being put through extreme temperatures to purify it, and finally being forged into the finished product, you too are being separated, purified and forged into a product; a personality, a vessel that will make proper use of that faith object, so that it benefits yourself and others when you finally *receive* it.

More importantly, you are receiving spiritual guidance and practical experience, progressing toward being a more productive faith son and daughter of the Heavenly Father. You are beginning to live the religion 'of' Christ Jesus; learning to apply the measure of faith that you have been given by *directing* it in the fulfilling of GOD's Will and purpose for your life.

It should be observed that, objects seem to be received more readily when they are for a genuine need, such as for food and shelter, and when they are of a spiritual nature, such as for knowledge, understanding and wisdom, and for the discernment of truth, beauty and goodness. Things of spirit value are more readily forthcoming than when faith is applied for material things to fulfill some desire or want. Your faith object is also more readily received when the object is not specifically for your benefit alone, or for your benefit at all. But you may also receive it sooner if you ready to receive it sooner, if you have already been prepared. GOD the Father knows when it is the appropriate *point-in-time* for you to receive the object(s that you are hoping to receive.

Institutional religions and their followers assert that human beings on earth somehow have special favor with the Heavenly Father because Christ Michael, His begotten Son one of them was bestowed in this world as Christ Jesus of Nazareth. They presuppose that His coming to this sphere called earth was just so the human race occupying this planet can have the opportunity of being saved from damnation, but being more realistic, being saved from extinction. Well...that's part of the plan, but just a very small reason for the Creator Son of this universe coming to this planet. It would be extremely beneficial to your personal spiritual growth to discover some of the main reasons. What you find will truly expand your spiritual reality.

A byproduct of the effects of institutional religious doctrine is the arrogance and pride associated with its' belief system. If our Heavenly Father is as Holy and as pure and righteous as generally believed, *and He is*, and more so than we could possibly conceive, then it is completely unrealistic, illogical and unwise to believe that once we depart this earth, that we will somehow magically or mystically be so perfect as to be immediately ushered into the presence of the Universal Father.

Christ's blood, His wounds, His suffering, His death and His subsequent resurrection did much more than any human is even capable of comprehending, but it did not accomplish that...our perfection.

It is difficult and sometimes impossible to accept the truth, even to those who diligently search for it. But there are spiritual realities, truths that extend far beyond the scriptural information imparted through institutional religious teachings. And if the purveyors of these religious teachings actually know the truth, they certainly aren't going to share it with there congregations. For them to do so would be religious suicide. Ministers would have to seek another profession.

Yet another byproduct of institutional religious doctrine is that it elicits confusion in regard to what constitutes belief and what constitutes faith; what a person *believes* as it relates to and activates the other components of faith. It seems apparent that many people are of the notion that belief *is* faith. It is not! Belief is a necessary component of faith, and it is required for faith to work, but it is not faith altogether.

Faith is based on the foundation of universal truth, and that truth *'cannot'* be changed. Universal truth is perpetual, self-sustaining and permanent, and truth provides the building blocks for everything that is materially real and spiritually real. Universal truth and individual truth is relative. It is relative to the subject matter it pertains to, or that is in question. Individual truth for one person is not necessarily the truth for another. Receiving that which is the truth for you, is based upon the experiences in your environments that you have adapted to and which has dictated your behavior over time, and based upon your beliefs and your ability to understand. More than these, the receiving of your faith object is based upon the amount of faith that is apportioned to you and your diligent application of it.

Faith is a spiritual tool and possessed by every free will being; it is a mechanism by which we can reach into the spiritual realm to access the benefits of being a son or daughter of GOD. It is the manner in which we maintain and sustain an ever constant, perpetual and lasting personal relationship with our Heavenly Father.

The story of the prodigal son has been told many times, being used in sermons by preachers and lessons by religious teachers. Usually, the story is focused on the youngest brother, but there's a story to be told about the older brother as well.

The story tells how the younger of two sons was generally care- free, shiftless and irresponsible. Then one day the youngest son goes to his Father and asks for all that was his inheritance. His Father, being a prosperous person of means, gives his son his inheritance and bids him farewell.

The older son was disturbed by this event, but feeling that he had done most of his younger brother's work anyway, quickly got over any resentment of his father giving the young son his due, as determined by their Father. He was really glad to see him go.

Not to belabor the story, the young man spent all of his inheritance and times got hard. His friends deserted him and he was reduced to contemplating eating food meant for the swine. Then after coming to his senses, remembering who he was, the son of a prosperous man, the young man decides to swallow his pride and arrogance and return home.

His father had been looking for him for some time, hoping that he would come back home; and then one day, while looking out over his land, he sees his son returning and commands the servants to prepare a feast in gladness of his son's homecoming.

As expected, when the oldest son discovered that his younger brother had returned and their father was preparing a big feast in his honor, he was not a happy person. He was so distraught in fact, that he went and questioned his father about it. He even pointed out the fact that he had been a faithful and responsible son, doing all that he, the Father had asked of him, and yet the father had never shown him favor in such a manner. Upon which the father replied; "all that I have is yours, and you could have done with it as you will at any time."

The message that is lost or neglected is the fact, the truth that all that the father had was already his sons to enjoy, both of them. Either or both of them could have received what they asked of their Father at any time. The disgruntled son simply neglected to do so. Whether from a lack of knowledge and understanding about his father's generosity, or whether out of the fear of being rejected, the story does not say, but either can deprive us of the truth that makes possible a great many things for us that are already ours for the asking.

People are subject to *believe* anything, whether true or not. What a person believes is not always founded in truth or even fact, although as a person seeking the true religion, your belief system should be... founded in truth. Simply *accepting* something as being true from a friend or even a minister does not make it true. People believe lies all the time. Con artist and scam artist rely on people readily believing lies. And they are very good at their practice of getting people to believe them. No spiritual or natural laws need apply for someone to *believe* something. That is their choice.

Truth is justified *in* faith, and faith is justified *by* truth. Truth provides the basis on which faith operates. It is the law of righteousness! And *truth based* faith is activated by *truth based* beliefs. The amount of belief you proffer and the work, the effort you exert or service you render qualifies and quantifies the extent of your sincerity. It expresses the true amount of hope, of expectation that you have for receiving the object(s of your directed faith.

Your sincere efforts and work also express to the Heavenly Father that you trust Him. You trust that His Word is dependable and true; and you trust that the Father's Will and purpose for your life is for your good despite the seeming negative environmental responses to your prayers and requests that you may encounter in the process.

Things just seem to stop going your way! Or your way as you perceive it. The immediate natural reactions, the unharmonious and often disheartening events that now occur in your experiences; the unexpected consequence that results from your obedience to the Spirit of GOD within you may truly be emotionally trying for a season. But you will endure, and this too will pass from your cold and uninspiring winter into your live and vibrant spring...almost unnoticeably.

This is an attitude that encourages and inspires gratitude and thanksgiving; knowing that even when we don't fully discern the guidance of our indwelling GOD Fragment and the leading by the Holy Spirit and our angelic Seraphic Guardians, when we don't get it quite right, the outcome will still be for our good.

In due time, you will be rewarded...spiritually, mentally, physically and materially. You will understand the urgings and promptings by the Spirit.

Your efforts, based on your ability and your capacity to understand, and your willingness to accept and apply the precepts of truth by the process of faith application, you begin to acknowledge and understand that because you are within the kingdom of heaven, such practices will become as natural to you as refreshing rain that falls from the clouds on a hot summer day. So through every circumstance and situation learn to be grateful; being thankful in everything, for such is the Father's Will in Christ Jesus concerning you.

THE INSPIRED WORD OF GOD

From the time of my birth, and as far back as I can remember, my family was associated with a church of the Baptist denomination, and the same church. At that time, it was a very small church with a small congregation of between one hundred to one hundred and fifty people. It was located in the township of Spencer or Choctaw, Oklahoma. To this day I don't know which town it was actually located in because the boundaries separating the two seemed to not be well defined except to those actually living near or within their borders.

My immediate family, my parents and siblings as well as our grandparents, and other relatives along with many of our classmates and friends from school and work with whom our parents associated also attended the small church. Some of the families even helped to build the little church, and were so close as friends that they were really considered our extended family.

As years passed and ministers came and went from the church, the deacons, deaconesses and board of trustees determined to find a more permanent pastor of the church...and they did. But not before having a great deal of controversy among the church membership. Nevertheless, a minister was finally accepted and shortly thereafter he began an outreach ministry with the intent of expanding the church in membership and providing a larger building in which to worship.

Under the leadership of the newly accepted pastor and after a relatively short period of time, the church did indeed grow, both in actual size through a building program and in membership through an extensive outreach ministry. This was achieved by witnessing to people in the immediate neighborhoods around the church and other communities in Oklahoma City as well.

After receiving some training, members of the church went two by two throughout various communities and neighborhoods in Spencer, Midwest City, Choctaw and Oklahoma City, witnessing to the people; doing their best to follow the example as they believed it to be of Christ Jesus as He and the Apostles and disciples had done as they traveled throughout Israel and the regions around about, spreading the gospel, the good news of the kingdom.

The doctrine and principles regarding Christian behavior and conduct which the small church adopted were in accordance with the standards of the National Baptist Congress or Convention, and was called the church covenant. This covenant was recited every first Sunday of the month following the baptism of new members and after members partook of the communion which represented the body and blood of Christ Jesus.

These rituals were always considered sacred because they were believed to be in accordance with biblical scripture; as being part of the Last Supper that Jesus had with His twelve Apostles shortly before He was crucified. The then growing church followed the scripture almost to the letter as it was written in their religious doctrine.

The pastor, a devout and sincere man, genuinely concerned with the religious development and growth of the church's members, seemed to understand that there must also be personal material growth also... at least to a degree; a degree that would meet people's basic needs. He was very astute and knew that otherwise, their focus would just be on their immediate material and physical needs rather than the message he was attempting to deliver.

As most ministers do, He used the *Bible* and taught it as being *the Word of GOD*, using it as his road map, his guide. The church pastor was attempting to portray the behavior of Christ, demonstrating how Jesus by feeding the hungry, healing the sick, and performing other miracles, brought people to believe and trust in Him as the Messiah. By helping to relieve some of the peoples' basic needs, Jesus' concepts and precepts of truth were more readily received by many people. Jesus presented the true gospel of the kingdom to His listeners and gained many disciples, believers and followers in the process.

Forthwith, the church pastor began a building program and established an outreach mission in Oklahoma City. The church began feeding those who were hungry and established clothes closet for those in need of clothes, and provided shelter for the homeless to some extent, the extent to which the church could afford at that time.

Sunday mornings began with a gathering of the brotherhood, the deacons of the church, and that was followed by Sunday School. The deaconesses held their circle meetings in their homes, alternating between the homes of the sisterhood. It was in these settings along with the regular Sunday services where we learned the interpretations *of* biblical scripture and other religiously related materials.

Using Sunday School lesson books that were purchased from religious bookstores, the teachers would have each person who was willing, read a portion of the lesson's text for that Sunday, and then the reader would render their interpretation of what they had read. It was interesting to note how each one usually had a different interpretation of the reading; albeit, after a period of discussion most people seemed to agree with the teacher's or the text book's interpretation. They *conformed*, even if the teacher's interpretation and the interpretation of Scripture given in the text book was different from what they understood it to mean.

But that didn't prevent the teacher from doing their best to explain or interpret the scripture that was read, usually trying to illustrate how it applied to our lives at the time; and most often without success, because it simply wasn't practical or applicable to those more modern times.

The circumstances, situations, and the personalities and events portrayed in biblical scripture existed in the days in which the scriptures were written or within a few hundred years thereafter and such scriptures were not applicable then nor in the time in which we now live. The religious, social, political and economic environments are very different now than they were in the days when Christ lived among men. So, try as they did, those determined teachers could not reconcile the past with the present.

Without the truth, the whole picture, people will never be able to reconcile even the parts of the Bible that 'are' true, so that they can be practically applied to their lives today. Could that be because we have a misguided understanding about the Bible? Could it be because what we have been given in Scripture is but part of the story...a very small part? The answer is yes! to both questions!

For the longest time, the Bible has been heralded as the "Word of GOD," the so called "*inspired* Word of GOD." Battles have been fought and wars have been waged in defense of this supposedly sacred book, and scores of atrocities were inflicted upon people by Roman, Spanish and others in their efforts to force and impose their Bible based beliefs and doctrines upon helpless individuals and groups.

In earlier times only those within the priesthood of the Judaic religion and clerics of the Christian religion were allowed to even read the sacred scrolls and books that contained the writings that have since become known as the Bible. Even today, people think that they are being disloyal to GOD the Father if they even think to accept or to read other materials. How foolish!

The fact, the truth that there are a variety of versions of the Bible should be a clue that men are responsible for the contents of the Bible. It seems that the ultimate intent and purpose of biblical scripture as it is written, taught and learned today is subjugation and bondage to conformity; conformity to their interpretations of Scripture and to their belief systems.

But that's not being disloyal! It *is* being disloyal to the Heavenly Father and untruthful when you ascribe to Him, GOD the Father, things that are the works of men; and conversely, when you ascribe to men the things that are of and from GOD. It is very disloyal to the Father when people exploit Him as a means of material gain. The Bible falls into the former category. It is also being disloyal to GOD when you neglect to seek the truth, and allow people, whether they are ministers, preachers or others to influence and convince you that things which are untrue are of divine origin.

Not only is it disloyal to the Father, but there is also a real and present danger in doing so, because to be deceived into thinking that something is true in this case the Bible, as being the Word of GOD, when it is not, will most certainly lead you down the path to perpetual deprivation and possible destruction and away from the truth; away from Jesus the Christ, "the Way, 'the Truth' and the Life."

It is a lazy and slothful person that finds it easier to conform to the beliefs of others, rather than to seek the truth for themselves. They are content to abide in fantasies, half truths and lies because it doesn't require them to be courageous and fearless, stepping outside the boundaries of their comfort zone to discover the Heavenly Father's Will and purpose for their life. Instead, they prefer to submit to someone else's will and purpose for their life; someone who may or may not have their best interest at heart. Instead, they swallow the interpretations of Scripture that is based on someone else's experiences, as *they* believe it to mean; and that may or may not be true interpretations. But don't take my word for it, seek the truth for yourself!

But what does that mean anyway…the *inspired* Word of GOD? Those whose writings grace the books and the Psalms in what has become known as the Bible, supposedly either had spiritual revelations by the GOD of this universe or other celestial beings whom in their primitive and superstitious minds they considered to be GOD.

Prophets and prophetesses received revelations and prophecies either by personal visitations or by other means of communication, as through visions or a strong imparting of messages from their indwelling GOD Fragment.

These writers were 'inspired' to pen what they saw or heard; to write down and put to papyrus, sheepskin or some other material, those things which were revealed to them or which they believed were instructions and revelations. And sometimes they *actually* were inspired or instructed by these Beings of the Heavenly host to write.

To be *inspired* simply means to be "aroused, animated or to be imbued within their spirit to do something; to be motivated by supernatural or divine influence." A visit from a celestial being or a vision would certainly qualify as motivating factors, events that would inspire someone to write what they were being instructed to write or to write what they saw.

People of those days were eager to please and appease the gods. The people doing the writing were in possession of primitive, superstitious and fearful minds and ever wary of spirits, whether perceived to be friendly or unfriendly. They were disinclined to disobey for fear of unpleasant repercussions. Genuine Spirit guidance as most people believed them to be in those days, gave way to embellished fantasies and their own experiences and beliefs which became part of what was being written.

Unfortunately, primitive thinking and believing people are still abundant today. During the period in which the Bible was written, those kinds of occurrences apparently happened frequently, and today scholars of religion and language have sought to correct obvious flaws and inconsistencies, attempting to give more meaning and relevance to biblical scripture; making it even more the "words of men."

There are lots of *inspired* writings in the sixty six books of the Bible that most Christian denominations use. Within these sixty-six books are commands, instructions, prophecies, stories, and warnings of punishment and promises of rewards. But there is also pure embellished fiction contrived by men with other than righteous motives; all meant to encourage, to guide and direct, to inspire, and mostly to frighten the reader or hearer into conformity to the traditional religious beliefs and practices of *those* times. In particular, to conform to the beliefs, rituals and ceremonial practices of one group of people, the Jewish people, the Hebrews and those gentiles who chose to convert to Judaism, the religion of the Hebrews, and later to convert people to Christianity after the death and resurrection of Christ.

The Hebrew people had come to adopt strict religious disciplines by which to live. They had come to accept the concept and belief in one GOD, YAHWEH as the GOD of Israel. This was one of several reasons that Christ Michael selected this group of people through whom He would live out His mortal life as a human being, as Jesus of Nazareth.

With the approval of GOD the Paradise Father and the assistance of His Celestial Brethren, Michael the Sovereign GOD and Creator of this universe and all that there is in it, selected these people from among all the races of earth to be the torch bearers of truth and light. And it is in that context '*only*' that the term "chosen people" should be applied to the Jewish people. Remember, GOD the Father is no respecter of persons nor people. Indeed, they yielded up that prominent distinction and honor when they persisted in their dogmatic traditions and rejected the new gospel of the kingdom of heaven which Christ Jesus came to proclaim.

In their ignorance and self righteousness, they failed to recognize the Son of Man as the true SON of GOD, the Truth, the Way and the Life who walked among them teaching the precepts of GOD the Father's spiritual kingdom. In their arrogance and greed, and in their rigid and unrelenting self righteousness they caused

Him to be crucified. But neither they nor the Romans killed Christ Jesus, the incarnate person of Michael, GOD's Creator Son. The creation cannot kill or destroy its Creator. They could only bring about the events that led to Him *laying down* His life.

So, there should be no hatred, malice or ill will held against the Jewish or Hebrew people. Would you be so selfrighteous, arrogant and proud as were the Pharisees, Sadducees and scribes in rejecting the truth, in rejecting Jesus if He was in the world today? Many people already do.

GOD the Father and Christ Michael His Creator Son, the GOD of *this* universe is not a respecter of any one particular group of people, nor is He a respecter of any person, that is; neither the Father nor the Son prefers one race or group of people above another. The Father loves each of us the same, with unconditional love, a love that is seldom understood by human beings because of their perverted concept of what love is. But the very fact and truth of our continued existence should bear witness to the kind of love the Father has for His sons and daughters. We don't *have* to be here!

Within the Bible there are curiosities, little gaps and not so little gaps where it seems something was intentionally left out or omitted; interestingly arranged phrases, and vague references to personalities such as Melchizedek and the Ancients of Days, as well as certain events that are out of context with the scriptural message or event being addressed. Even things like those related to the creation of the world and mankind as it is described or expressed in the Bible are not without peculiarities that the observant person can't help but notice. If they are wise, they will question these things. These things represent at least, inconsistencies that should cause the keen observer to pause and say "what?"

A seeker of the truth and a diligent student of biblical scripture most certainly detect these things…almost at a glance. As you give due diligence to interpretations being taught as doctrine in religious schools and in churches, these biblical curiosities, however vague a reference they may be, give way to serious contemplations about how those things could have been. Something doesn't quite ring true!

So, your search begins to try to fill in some of those gaps, seeking to discern the truth behind these inconsistencies and obvious omissions because you already perceive that, surely, the Word of GOD is both *true* and *consistent* or should be. When once the search begins, it almost immediately produces enlightenment and revelations that the Spirit of Truth discerns within and brings forth previously unknown and unspoken truths; truths that begin to expand your awareness of a spiritual reality of which few people are privy. Not because that truth is forbidden, prohibited or unobtainable, but because it was early kept from the general public, leaving the clergy's interpretation of Scripture as the only way to obtain biblical knowledge, but not so much, spiritual knowledge.

Many people today still have limited truth about spiritual reality, knowledge and understanding in regard to the spiritual liberty they truly possess; truths that remains hidden and untold by crafty and evil men with evil ulterior motives. They thought it best not to make public the real truth lest people would come to realize who they truly are as children of GOD the Paradise Father and not need them anymore.

Truth is made available to those who seek it and who are capable of employing *objectivity* by human reason and spiritual faith. Truth springs forth when one is capable of keeping an open mind to just the possibility that new information might very well be true. Truth is made available to those who are willing and capable of receiving, acknowledging and accepting the reality of the *real* 'Word of GOD,' Christ Jesus of Nazareth; and He does not need anyone other than the Spirit of GOD (our indwelling Spirit), and the Spirit of Himself the Spirit of Truth to reveal the truth in all matters, spiritual or otherwise.

When you begin to read biblical scripture yourself and stop relying on the preachers' interpretations and guidance, and when you allow the Spirit of GOD within *you* and the Spirit of Truth to reveal the truth, only then will you progress in your spiritual development, in your ability to understand and experience these truths. Only then will you know the truth and be made free to exercise your faith based on truth; and as you do, you will experience an ever increasing measure of faith being apportioned to you.

You only have to read the first few chapters of Genesis to discover the first curiosity and odd happenings. Beside the indication that there were two creations of man, there is the puzzling creation concept that Adam and Eve were the first human beings, that they were the first created man and woman. So, if they were the first two humans, where did the people that Cain was afraid would kill him come from?

After killing his brother Abel, Cain was banished and sent away from Adam and Eve, who, if literally interpreted from scripture were now the only two other people alive. According to the Bible he was punished by becoming a fugitive and a vagabond. He went to the land of Nod where he married a native woman of the land, and the story continues. But of what people was he afraid? Where did the people of Nod come from? Weren't there only the four people at the time... well, three after Abel was killed? If one interpreted the scripture as it is written, one would be confused. But there is much more to the story and you would be amazed to discover the real truth.

There are yet other vague references to Beings that the Bible does not elaborate on. The mysterious Melchizedek who is mentioned at least twice in the Bible, along with the Most High who people of those days and in ours erringly believe to be referencing GOD the Father, when in reality, they are other orders of the Sons of GOD. The Melchizedek's come forth from association with the Universe Creative Mother Spirit and the Father Melchizedek Son, the first Melchizedek created by our local universe Creator and Father and the Creative Mother Spirit; they come down to the inhabited worlds of His Universe in time and space as teachers of righteousness. These various Sons of GOD perform many functions in their efforts to minister to all the sons and daughters of GOD, all of the intelligent created beings seeking to ascend to GOD the Paradise Father.

Sometimes, it was difficult for the inspired revealer of revelations, and other tellers of stories and purveyors of guidance to express the messages that they received and believed that they were being told to impart to people; to many who had a limited capacity of understanding. They used words and symbols that the people of those time periods could relate to and understand.

You should not doubt that embellishments were used to impart the principles and doctrines received in visions and visitations to facilitate the peoples' understanding. Writers do it frequently to maintain interest in and enhance the material they are writing. They often used metaphors also to make it easier to comprehend by everyone, things that the people could readily relate to.

Moses must have had an incredibly difficult task, trying to penetrate the barriers of long ingrained pagan beliefs that existed in the minds of the Israelites and gentiles coming from under four hundred years of bondage to the Pharaohs in Egypt. He had to use language and symbols, illustrations and portrayals that they could understand to help them overcome the slavery mindset which bondage had conditioned them with, and to impart the concept of one GOD to them and establish a firm trust and belief in the one true living GOD.

But the methods of teaching, relaying information and instructions to people of Moses' time, many who may have had limited education and knowledge, leaves much room for misinterpretation by people of a much later time...our time.

Moses was attributed with having written the first five books of the Bible, called the Pentateuch. Together with other scriptural interpretations that were written and spoken as the oral teachings by the early Jewish people, were called the Talmud. These books the Jewish people cherished and held sacred, and many Israelites performed the rituals and worshipped in accordance with what was written in them. These rituals, traditions and methods of worshipping GOD became Jewish or Hebrew law. Some continued to practice their traditions even after they were again taken into captivity and threatened with death if they continued to practice them.

As you know, the Israelites spent a lot of time after their departure from Egypt either wandering around in the desert or being taken into captivity. Many still dogmatically revere these books as GOD's Law, even to this day, when in truth they were Moses' laws, not GOD's.

Then, in the first century following the death, resurrection and ascension of Christ Jesus, soldiers of the Roman empire demolished Jerusalem and began a campaign to kill those who professed to be Christians. They persecuted many who practiced this new and increasingly pervasive religion called Christianity, pitting them against lions, other slaves and Roman soldiers in their coliseum.

The written materials that were not hidden by the Jews or burned by the Roman soldiers were taken to Rome, confiscated in an attempt to suppress this new religion which the empire perceived as a threat.

Still, the Apostle *Paul's* version of Christianity flourished. So much so that it became a thorn in the side of Roman Emperors for several centuries after Christ's ascension. There were times when persecution under Roman Emperors came close to decimating the ranks of those claiming Christianity as their religion. Many Roman emperors such as Nero around AD 64, Marcus Aurelius between AD 165 180, and especially Diocletian and his Caesar Galerius about AD 303, were brutal in their attempts to abolish the new religion. It wasn't until the rule of Constantine the Great that Rome adopted Christianity as its religion during the 4th century AD.

Nevertheless, if the Roman Empire was not killing Christians, it was inculcating and distorting the true religion with their pagan beliefs and practices. Many practices like Easter with the traditional Easter egg hunt and Christmas have become firmly grounded in the Christian religion of today. People would be surprised to discover that Christ Jesus was not born on December the 25th, but rather on August 21st, 7 B.C.; and that they are actually paying homage to the sun god of early Roman worshipers when they celebrate Christmas.

Under the Roman Emperor Constantine, the council of Nicaea was convened to determine and clearly define what the core beliefs of the Christian religion would be. This council was commissioned to decide which surviving Jewish manuscripts, written and oral history of the Jewish people would be imposed upon the people; basically, what teachings the Bible would contain. It's all a matter of history!

Yes, *men* determined what books, writings, doctrine and principles would become the guiding beacon of Christianity and some of them were not even godly men. This book would be the means by which they would rule and control the world, by controlling the minds and hearts of the people. And there is no more effective way to accomplish this than through religion. If you can control what a person believes... you can control them. And what more effective way of getting people to believe something than to label it "the Word of GOD?"

Be that as it may...why the history lesson? Just to point out that men were responsible for literally writing and editing the Bible...not GOD!!! Men decided what went in and what was omitted from the book; and they determined what other contents should appear and not appear in the Bible, any version of the Bible, and in this period of time there are many different versions. Men are fallible and often unscrupulous. It is often difficult to know the motives of a person who *outwardly* appears holy or righteous; one seldom knows what inspires them and what their true intentions are.

Please! Let me make this abundantly clear! I am not discounting the Bible or its content, because despite all of the above, the Bible still contains much truth; although the Spirit of Truth must earnestly be relied on to discern those truths. We must trust that our Heavenly Father would not leave us without some *initial* means, some way of making Himself knowable to us human beings. Even so, the Spirit of Truth and the Spirit of our Father that dwells within our mind would reveal the truth about the spiritual reality, the kingdom of heaven; and He does reveal the truth to us when we allow Him to do so.

The true *'Word of GOD'* is revealed to you and to me, and to everyone who can recognize it, by His Spirit that dwells within our heart and mind. It is a personal revealing of His truth to us, for us. It is a true personal religious experience.

Nevertheless, if it were proven that the Bible was fake, biblical scripture would still be relevant and pertinent in our search to know GOD the Father. It would have served the most important objective of any supposed holy scripture; that of turning the hearts and minds of the human race to GOD the Universal Father, GOD the Eternal Son the *real* WORD of GOD, and to GOD the Infinite Spirit. These three Deity Personalities comprise the Paradise Trinity.

Looking at the Bible in the context of the bigger picture, the Bible can be seen as a window through which is witnessed the spiritual evolution of religion. Religion, like people has *evolved. Evolution* is simply the further development of people or things over a period of time; changing something from one state of being to a more advanced or progressive state of being. Evolution dictates that life and the things associated with life are always progressively moving forward and upward with the goal of attaining *perfection.*

While there are other reference materials that provide more insightful information, and that presents clearer and deeper truths depicting the religious development of human beings, the Bible does illustrate how the Lord GOD at certain times elevated the religious experiences of the Jewish people, but it does not so much explain how by faith mankind is to become more spiritually developed.

At a certain time after the concept of worship had been adopted, some religions began to focus the attention of their cultures toward the notion of one GOD. The Heavenly Father allowed fear and retribution to be used as a means to divert mankind's worship and praise away from idol gods made of wood and stone, and instead redirecting their belief to the One True GOD.

A Melchizedek, a Descending Son of the Sovereign GOD of the Universe, was a teacher of righteousness and life skills who was on earth at the time of Abraham, selected him and began developing the concept of faith through Abraham, who is scripturally called, Father of the faithful. The Christian and Judaic belief is that through Abraham, specifically, by the faith that he exercised, all of humanity can be adopted into the family of GOD the Father. But by faith those who seek truth and employ their faith as best they know how, and those who seek the kingdom of GOD, were sons and daughters of GOD even before Abraham. They were already sons and daughters of GOD in the Mind of GOD in eternity, where time is of no consequence other than the mechanism by which humanity progresses to perfection. His thoughts and His Will are already manifested and done in eternity. It is now a matter of only being played out on the stages of time and space.

You can see religious concepts further developing, evolving as you observe how the Father of this universe dealt with Moses and the children of Israel; allowing them to be taught by the method of reward and punishment; which through Moses' laws when obeyed supposedly led to prosperity and well being, and when disobeyed led to destruction, captivity and a state of 'not so well being.'

We see religion further evolve to the revelation of the Truth being incarnated on earth in the form of Christ Jesus of Nazareth. His revolutionary expression of GOD's Love for all of His creation; His teachings and sayings, many of which has been concealed until this point in time, the end of the age. When these new or concealed truths are revealed and acknowledged they unveil a spiritual kingdom in which all of humanity participates or they can.

It is a kingdom in which by using *faith* based on the precepts of truth, human beings have the capacity to abundantly thrive and prosper. This spiritual evolution is going on today; and in the due course of time, it will replace these religions which require group participation and communal conformity as their means of worship, transplanting in their place a truer revelation and deeper conviction to know the truth and to know GOD's Will and doing it. However, it requires our diligent efforts to seek the Father's Will and know the truth, discovering and developing our own individual and personal form of praise and worship.

CHRISTIANS AND JESUSONIANS DEFINED

Christianity began with Paul the Apostle and Peter the Apostle of Christ Jesus. After Paul's conversion on the Road to Damascus, he began teaching about *his* spiritual experience. If you know the story then you may be aware that before Paul's experience on the road to Damascus he was a persecutor of Christians and the Christian Churches that were in their beginning stages. Paul was a Roman citizen but he was a staunch believer in Judaic law; the Mosaic laws by which the Sanhedrin courts adjudicated religious violations. He was tenacious in pursuing violators of the laws and bringing them before the Sanhedrin court.

You have probably heard the story of how Peter denied knowing Jesus three times after the Roman soldiers arrested Christ. This same Peter did indeed establish the first Christian Church in Jerusalem shortly after the death, resurrection and ascension of Christ Jesus, and James the brother of Jesus became the head of this church. Contrary to belief, James was the full blood brother of Christ Jesus, yet he was not an apostle of Christ's.

Much of the Christian church's doctrine today is predicated on the letters of Paul to the various churches throughout Asia and other areas of the Middle East. In reality, churches to this day seem to value Paul's teachings above those of the Master, Christ Jesus. In fact and in truth there are very few teachings of Christ Jesus in the Bible. Especially when you consider that the four gospels according to Matthew, Mark, Luke and John are really their accounts of what they heard Christ say and saw Him do; these accounts were how they remembered His life and teachings as conditioned by their own personal experiences with Him. Some of these accounts were written many years after the events happened and were recorded by themselves and others as best they could be remembered.

These four testaments by some of His Apostles and disciples tell of the exploits and teachings of Jesus the Christ, expressing the accounts of the events and interactions of Jesus with Jews and Gentiles. Those Apostles giving their testimony about the works and teachings of Christ Jesus were all according to their recollection and from their perspective.

Not to discredit Paul or his letters, because they contain much truth. But these letters were meant for the particular churches being established or already established in the cities to whom the letters were addressed and to the people who lived there. His letters were meant to provide guidance and to set moral standards for those specific people and churches according to *his* beliefs about the Master and *his* concepts of morality. His letters were in accordance with *his* perspectives of the new religion based on his personal spiritual experiences.

Still, they were *his* experiences; a personal transformation of purpose, but not so much a transformation of behavior. Paul was always assertive and driven; motivated by strict Judaic religious beliefs. But there was a change in the man which was preceded by his supposed encounter with Jesus on the road to Damascus. It was that event that put his actions into overdrive, motivating him to establish churches all throughout the Roman Empire. Their empire was firmly established in power at the time.

Paul was a powerful force in the spreading of his perceptions of what a believer and follower of Christ should be, and he was the major developer and propagator of the Christian Faith as it exists today. Even in biblical scripture it can be seen that Peter and Paul had conflicting ideas about how the doctrine of Christian Churches should be perceived, and what should be required of new converts.

Paul did prevail however. But in doing so, much of the teachings of Christ Jesus our Master were omitted or discarded. The teachings of Jesus where also compromised by Greek and Roman beliefs and practices, which up to that point in time the Father allowed so that the religion could grow and take its natural course in human spiritual development; with the primary objective being to get people to believe in GOD the Father and in Christ Jesus His Son; accepting them and being born again into His Kingdom as His children.

But it is not Paul through which our deliverance and assurance of survival has come. We have few who can attest to Paul's works or his credibility, other than Paul himself, Luke and perhaps Barnabas and Timothy. Although in the Bible, the book of Acts is entitled; The Acts of the Apostles, only the acts of a few of Christ Jesus' Apostles are included. Mostly, the book of Acts is about the acts and the experiences of Paul.

Certainly, Paul's teachings are of great merit in regard to moral behavior, yet, it was not him or his teachings upon which the church was to be founded. When Christ Jesus asked: "Who do men say that the Son of man is?" and then after receiving various replies, He asked, "But who do you say that I am?" and Simon Peter answered, "Thou art the Christ, the Son of the living GOD." It is written that Christ Jesus declared: "Blessed art thou, Simon Barjonah: for flesh and blood hath not revealed it unto you, but my Father who is in heaven. And I also say unto you, *that thou art Peter, and upon this rock I will build my church; and the gates of Hell shall not prevail against it.*"

According to biblical scripture, the church was to be founded on Simon Peter, and he did indeed found the first Christian Church in Jerusalem, but this church was founded on the doctrine and the truth regarding the resurrection of Jesus, His life, the miracles He performed and some of His teachings as *Peter* understood them. This being said, the rock upon which Christ's Church was to be built, the rock that Christ Jesus was referring to, was not a literal building to be called a church, but rather, the rock was the foundation of truth that was revealed to Peter; the truth that Christ Jesus was, and still is the Son of GOD, and all the knowledge, understanding and wisdom that comes with this revelation is yours as you accept Them for who They truly are.

Christianity was and continues to be a religion that is' about' Jesus; describing very few of the events that actually took place in His life. Special attention is given to his purported miracles, and his telling of parables and some of His interactions with specific people of that day.

Nevertheless, Christianity is based on writings as they were recalled and remembered by those who actually witnessed these events or by others who heard about them.

Such is the Christian religion of today, having its roots, its traditions and faith as it existed in its early beginnings, in yesterday. Religion is only today evolving into its true form, and Christianity in particular is devolving. As more people come to realize that the source of the emptiness, the sense of spiritual deprivation and the void within still remains, even after Sunday worship. The traditional religious repetitive rituals and ceremonies continue. Christianity requires no real commitment to GOD the Father. It stresses devotion to the church, the building and the people who frequent it. Religion has early been fashioned into a religion in which people can commit all sorts of heinous acts against their fellow human beings, against society and most of all against GOD the Father. Many people who profess to be Christians think that all they need do is to confess their deeds, their sins without truly being repentant- and everything will be forgiven and they can go on living their ungodly lives. Their disillusionment is forthcoming!

Gradually truth seekers will step out, really step out on faith and attain the level of individual spiritually effective faith that practitioners of the true religion elicits. But today Christianity continues to emphasize the acts of Christ Jesus. It is a religion that is mostly 'about' Him, giving very little recognition and adherence to the Spirit driven faith and practices 'of ' Jesus. For that would require being born again; having a change of mind, belief systems and behavior towards others.

Christianity today is the end result of the corrupting of the teachings of Christ Jesus by incorporating many pagan beliefs of the Greeks and Romans into Christ's original teachings. This Christianity does not truly convey that GOD the Father is our Paradise Father and that all of the created beings in this universe and all others are sons and daughters of this same Father.

This Christianity does not offer the knowledge or produce the understanding that comes from acknowledging and accepting the truth, and the fact that real personal spiritual experiences, the things that produce real *spirit value* come by the applying of one's faith. It is not a requisite of Christianity that one becomes a truth seeker who wholeheartedly believes that they are inheritors of GOD's kingdom; believing and trusting so much that they be absolutely confident in that knowledge by faith. In Christianity it is not necessary to acknowledge GOD the Universal Father as our Heavenly Father or realize and respect the honor and privilege that the Father has bestowed on us as His son or daughter.

It is not my intentions to try to discredit or downplay the role that Christianity has played in the advance toward spiritual perfection of the inhabitants of this world, or to minimize the importance of actually '*reading*' biblical scripture for one's self. For there is written on the pages of the Bible many truths and much wisdom and guidance, and beautiful works that can be attributed to those who wrote them. Hopefully, you will not become disenchanted or discouraged from anything that is written within these pages. Rather, let these writings spark a sense of urgency within your heart and mind to question some of the doctrine and principles that you have come to accept unquestionably and unequivocally as truth and fact and as the '*Word of GOD.*'

Begin to research for yourself the things that you may have from time to time found to be curious; things that you just could not quite reconcile within your mind by common sense, logical reasoning, or by the answers you may have received from the clergy or others who claim knowledge of religious or spiritual matters.

If you have read the Bible as you would read a book, and not in segments, surely you have certainly found such things. And when you perhaps have asked questions regarding them, you may have been told something like, "Oh! That's a matter of faith!

Some things you just gotta' take on faith and not question GOD;" or maybe you were told that, "some things are not meant for us to know;" or something similar.

To those things I say…rubbish!!! When you pray, don't you *ask* for wisdom, *knowledge* and understanding? Without asking questions and sincerely *seeking* the truth of a matter, how can you possibly *find* and know the answers to your questions?

Remember!!! It is written that Christ Jesus said: "Ask, and it shall be given you; seek, and you shall find; knock, and it shall be opened unto you." Christ also said: "If ye (you) abide in **My word**, *then* are you truly **My disciples**; and you shall know the *truth*, and *the truth* shall make you free."

There are a lot of Paulians; those who call themselves Christians. But they are really adherers of a compromised religious belief system; a system nearly devoid of the teachings of Christ Jesus; and they have been denied until now anyway knowledge of *all* the events of His life among mortals as a mortal Himself; that is, except for a small account of His words found in the four Gospels of the New Testament. And they wonder why their prayers seem to go unanswered, and why the faith that they try to apply and practice is ineffective. They wonder why they seem to have become stagnant and unprogressive in their spiritual growth; why they feel as though they are presenting a façade of piousness when they try to tell others 'about' the Master, Christ Jesus, perceiving that there is more that they should know… and there is!

The *Jesusonian brotherhood and sisterhood* is yet in the early stages of their spiritual development. They are the brothers and sisters of all races of human beings who first seek the Kingdom of GOD, knowing that when they have found and profess GOD that they have also found His righteousness; and they do this by loving the Lord their GOD with all of their heart, and with all their mind and strength.

They believe that love for and loyalty to the Heavenly Father is exemplified by their earnest and sincere pursuit to know Him and attempt to do His Will. Albeit, there is very little that is revealed in biblical scripture; that which is revealed to them as an individual, personally; but particularly, His Will as it is revealed to them by their indwelling Mystery Monitor, and His Will as found in the *Urantia Book*.

Jesusonians live and act by faith when the Will of the Father is not known; proceeding as though the object of their faith is His Will for them to obtain, and they patiently await His guidance through the many ministering spirits that assist in our progress and ascension to Paradise. Jesusonians diligently seek truth, beauty and goodness. They adhere to His advance preparation of them so they can receive and better manage their faith object. They have come to understand that one method that the Father uses to guide those seeking to apply their faith is by allowing doors to open or close to reveal His Will. They surrender their will to the Will of the Father so that He may hone the faith that He gave them, so they may be effective in obtaining their prosperity and be ministers who offer aid to others.

Jesusonians seek to really find and experience genuine love for themselves. Love that leads them to self-realization, and that allows them to truly love their neighbor, their brothers and sisters as they love themselves. They seek to do unto others as they would have others do unto them. They sincerely and without reservation try to demonstrate their love through selfless service, expecting nothing in return from those who benefit from their service. By faith, Jesusonians expect an open storehouse from GOD the Father, GOD the First Source and Center.

Jesusonians seek true spiritual enlightenment; they seek the truth, and rely on the Spirit of Truth, the Spirit of Christ Jesus to discern the truth by giving them assurance that the matter that they perceive as truth is either indeed truth or it is not.

They have experienced some method of confirmation that affirms truth when it is revealed. They understand that truth comes from many sources and they are ever vigilant to discern that truth as it is revealed.

Jesusonians are the natural spiritual evolution of Christianity. They are those who endeavor to learn as much about our Creator as has been revealed, and that will continue being revealed. They understand that the purpose of Christ Jesus coming to this world was to reveal the true nature, attributes and character of GOD the Universal Father, and to also reveal the nature, attributes, character, and faith potentials of humans to the Heavenly Father.

Jesusonians do not attempt to live the life of Christ Jesus their Master. Rather, they attempt to live their own lives in accordance with the concepts and precepts of the Son of GOD as He lived and taught them. Jesusonians acknowledge their human nature; always maintaining hope that by having and applying faith, that in time, GOD the Father will overcome the character defects in them that He doesn't want His children to exhibit. They understand and believe that they are already forgiven for any and all transgressions, and that all that is necessary is to ask the Father for forgiveness; realizing that GOD's Grace and Mercy is infinitely sufficient to compensate for their experiences of succumbing to their natural instincts, which have no spirit value.

Jesusonians do not abuse that liberty, understanding that the true nature of sin is to knowingly and intentionally act against GOD's Will, and it is being disloyal and displaying blatant disregard for the Father's children and His Will.

Jesusonians endeavor to impart knowledge about the Kingdom of GOD and spiritual reality as each one of them personally understand the spiritual reality of the Father's Kingdom to be. They try to impart this knowledge with respect for their fellow brothers' and sisters' faith and their denominational or religious beliefs.

The Jesusonians impart their knowledge and truth to others only to the degree and extent to which others are willing to receive such knowledge and truth.

The most sincere desire of Jesusonians is to bring the Kingdom of GOD to earth as it is in heaven. They realize that this is accomplished by proclaiming the Truth as it is revealed to them and by acknowledging Beauty and portraying Goodness. They allow the Fruit of the Spirit to abide over them, endeavoring to let the Fruit of patience to gradually prevail and eventually manifest all of the Spirit's Fruits as their natural spiritual character traits and behavior.

THE EVOLUTIONARY TRUTH OF CREATION

It requires a degree of faith to believe in things that one does not   personally witness and experience; especially things that were written by people of earlier times that saw and recorded history with primitive mindsets, and whose writing was according to their customs and traditions, even if those things being written were not true. Many of the events recorded in the Bible were not even documented during the time periods in which they supposedly happened. They were not even documented by the ones that supposedly witnessed or participated in the events. It requires both courage and a greater degree of faith to believe a new truth, idea or concept after you have been conditioned for so long to believe otherwise.

"Then the Master proceeded to warn his hearers against entertaining the notion that all olden teaching should be replaced entirely by new doctrines. Said Jesus: "That which is old and also true must abide. Likewise, that which is new but false must be rejected. But that which is new and also true, have the faith and courage to accept. Remember it is written: 'Forsake not an old friend, for the new is not comparable to him. As new wine, so is a new friend; if it becomes old, you shall drink it with gladness.'"

Just because scholars and other notable people profess that something is truth doesn't make it so. And just because there is a wide or general consensus of agreement about a thing, doesn't make it true either.

Several years ago there were a number of televangelists, mostly fundamentalist, who weekly, *fervently* broadcast their beliefs about the creation and how the world, humankind and all of life on this sphere called earth came to be. They insisted that everything in this world and even the world itself was created in seven days. That notion was far from being theirs alone. It was and continues to be a belief that has been heralded in institutional religious denominations for millennia's and by millions of people.

Nevertheless, in more recent years these fundamentalist and others have apparently seen the folly and futility of their persistence of those notions and have relented at least to some degree. It is foolish to continue to believe a thing in which scientific truth has been undeniably proven.

Despite scientific verification and proof that this planet has been in existence for at least one billion years, many still hold fast to unrealistic notions. They cannot reconcile the notion that evolution and creation can and does co exist. Evolution is a part of creation. They are not separate and distinct events! Indeed, evolution continues, for it is an ongoing process of progression to a state of perfection.

Evolution is a matter of human progression as much as it is a matter of life progression. It is the progression of life from all of its various and previous forms; the changing of life forms from one state of being to another, to a more advanced state of existence. Albeit, the evolution of mankind from a physical point of view has reached its peak, and any further evolutionary development will be intellectual and spiritual.

Still, the arrogant and obstinate egos of many ministers, priest and parishioners disallows them to accept the truth. Especially concerning errant biblical scripture which they have read about and in their heart of hearts, and with plain old common sense they know could not have happened as it is recorded. But it's in the Bible!

Many witness the evidence and progress of evolution in some form all around them every day; still, they embrace the impractical and unrealistic fantasies and myths instead. They need not look too far back in time to see the process of evolution in progress.

Several years ago, I was working with a community development organization. A Minister in one of the local churches and I was on our way back home after seeing an assistant of the State Congressional Representative about a matter of concern. Except for a few occasional comments about what we thought we had achieved at the meeting we had ridden in relative silence.

As if to counteract the affects of the sleep I was rapidly about to embark upon, he posed a question to me. He asked, "Do you know the second verse in the first book of the Bible…Genesis?" I thought for a second, and then responded, "And the earth was without form, and void. And darkness was upon the face of the deep. And the Spirit of GOD moved upon the face of the waters."

He seemed somewhat surprised that I knew the verse but tried not to show it, commenting that; "few people that I've asked that question actually know the answer." He then remarked, "a *whole lot* happened between that first verse and the second verse of Genesis!" I asked, "What do you mean?" And he simply repeated what he had previously said. I gave *him* a bewildered look as *he* looked at the road ahead, seemingly confident that I would contemplate the matter further; and he was right!

Consider this, as I did! During the short time period of one century, the twentieth century in particular, the evolution of mankind in the acquiring of knowledge and the ability to apply this knowledge has propelled the world into the ever progressing state in which we now live. Mankind has taken a dramatic leap forward.

In a relatively short period of time, mankind has become so technologically advanced as to progress from the primitive forms of transportation used during all the centuries before and on into the 1800's; man progressed from using horses and carriages to using automobiles, airplanes and trains that reach incredible speeds.

Communications has evolved from the early stages of carrier services, evolving to communication capabilities that have gone from vacuum tube operated radios and television sets of the late 1940's and early 1950's, to the digitally operated and wireless cell phones and other electronic devices used today.

Advancements in medical technology has allowed for the increased life span capabilities of humanity well beyond those that were normally expected of humans in earlier centuries.

This too is evolution. And if the world and mankind can 'evolve' technologically, socially and even religiously as we have in even as short a time period as one or two hundred years, try to consider how it could and did evolve over the course of millions of years. The key element is *time*.

A form of evolution is witnessed with every event and experience of birth. Over a nine-month period of time give or take the fertilized seed produced through sexual activities of man and woman develops. That seed goes through several embryonic stages until the end result, a baby human being comes forth from the mother's womb. GOD the Father creates; human beings procreate.

So! Does the *truth of evolution* disqualify the *truth of creation*? It absolutely *does not!* Evolution is in truth a part of creation, or rather a part of the creative process!

Evolution as a part of creation takes a long *'time'* to unfold. It takes a long time for the end result of a concept to come to fruition. But it all begins with a creative idea; an idea that over time develops one step at a time from the concept or idea to the accumulation and gathering of necessary materials to bring about the *organization* of those materials into a form, a shape that is consistent with that creative idea. It always requires *'time'* and often repeated experiments, trials and errors in order to perfect, or at least, to make manifest a rudimentary yet operational version of that creative idea...a prototype.

What? Did you think that because something is created, that it instantaneously comes into existence? Perhaps this is an affect of this instant gratification attitude and behavior that people have always had. Even the most patient of us want to have something, whatever the something may be and we want it now.

Well...Happy to disillusion you! The truth tends to do that...it disillusions people. It takes time for processes involved with the discernment of truth to unfold and for confirmation to be made manifest. It takes time for that which we have come to believe to be dispelled by proven fact and confirmed truth. Now you must be patient, and rely on your faith in the Spirit of Truth to reveal and confirm spiritual truth as truth.

For example: It is a scientifically proven fact that dinosaurs and other prehistoric animals dominated parts of the world well before mankind made their appearance on this planet. Their bones are prominently displayed in many museums. It is a scientifically proven fact that there existed a primitive form of human being at certain times before and after most humans but not all were biologically uplifted by the Material Sons and Daughters of GOD, the Adams and Eves. Their whole purpose was to biologically upgrade mankind which would inevitably lead to our increased desire for spiritual enlightenment and material progress.

These are facts that are verified by visible and material evidence. There is much more proof available for those who earnestly desire to know the truth about mankind and the history of this sphere that we occupy; and there is even knowledge about the evolutionary creation of this universe.

Inevitably, if you seek truth you *will* find it. You will come to realize that there is a reality that is larger than the farthest horizons of perceived reality that now dominates our life experiences, and that anyone is capable of experiencing in this mortal life. It is a spiritually perceived reality that broadens our material, physical and increasingly, our spiritual dimensions to the extent that we can truly experience an abundant life and have lasting prosperity.

It is a reality about life that is in some ways like that lived by our Lord and Savior, Christ Jesus of Nazareth. That is after all what we should be striving for as sons and daughters of GOD the Universal Father. *You are striving for that... aren't you?*

For any person to try to exactly emulate the life of Christ is not possible, but we can obtain Christ consciousness; that which is called 'the mind of Christ.'

YOU ARE NEVER ALONE

That you have come to this point in the book is an indication that you at least find the material herein interesting or intriguing, but hopefully you have found it to be encouraging, enlightening and inspiring as well. If so, if you think that it has merit and that it is thought provoking enough, then perhaps you will consider the probability of the spiritual impact that the book's content can have in your life.

By opening up your mind to spiritual reality and becoming more aware of the much bigger picture, you should begin to realize that there is a lot more to faith than a mere superficial belief in GOD the Father and His Son Michael who became incarnate in the person of Christ Jesus. Without doubt, they are the way to eternal life. Yes, faith is that too, very much so, but it is much more.

There is a much bigger stage on which we are acting out the experiences of our mortal life, this physical and material reality in which we now live, and although you may think that you can live your life without the aid, assistance and companionship of your fellow human beings, your brothers and sisters, you are mistaken. Even more than the interaction that we experience with our fellow human beings, which we need to maintain our own identity and sanity, we need the aid and assistance of morontial and spiritual beings of the Heavenly host to guide, direct and protect us as we proceed along our journey in our quest for perfection.

Faith is a force and it is required to believe in the unseen things, the beings, and the *ministering spirits* that are ever by our side, and to believe in the unseen activities and events forever taking place in the spiritual realm to assist us as a faith son or daughter of GOD in our progression to perfection. These are things that you have never learned in Sunday school at church, or from the sermons preached by ministers every Sunday.

It requires a degree of faith and courage to go outside of conformity and step outside the confines of your comfort zone and question things that we have long been conditioned to believe and begin to seek enlightenment, to seek truth. Be assured that the Spirit of Truth that has already been poured upon you, you will receive; and it will be activated when you literally ask the Spirit of Truth, the Spirit of Christ Jesus to come into your heart. By inviting Him into your heart with such a request, He will come and abide with you and dwell within you and give you discernment of those things that *are* true. The Spirit of Truth, The Spirit of Christ Jesus was poured out *upon* all flesh on the day of Pentecost, but He still has to be invited into your heart and into your life.

The biggest confidence builder of human beings is the Spirit of Truth and the knowledge one gains from the Holy Spirit. Along with your divine Spirit Fragment, they purge from you the things that are error, and stimulates you to pursue the things of truth, beauty and goodness. Together, they help discern those things that are the truth as it relates to all things, and such knowledge and guidance will motivate you to act based on such guidance and knowledge.

This liberation giving knowledge, the truth by faith and unmerited grace releases you from the animal nature of the flesh; the things to which the flesh has become accustomed to doing and conditioned to do, and in some cases, things which human beings are expected to do; things which may or may not be sinful.

Sin, in the *dictionary* is defined as; "an act, thought, or way of behaving that goes against the law or teachings of '*a religion*', especially when the person who commits it is aware of what they are doing or intend to do." This may well be the definition of sin according to human concepts in regard to the religions of men, and by those who develop and practice the institutional doctrine of their particular religions and denominations, but this does not account for intentional and premeditated acts of going against the will of GOD the Father. There is a vast difference! For the things that men consider as religion and as sin are very seldom the same as how GOD the Father considers them.

Spiritually, and in the true religion, sin is defined as; an act, thought, or way of behaving that goes against the *will of GOD*, and continuing to do so is inequity. And it is of these willful and intentional sins that one must repent. To repent is an act of contrition, initially having a conscience laden with guilt that prompts one to be sincerely sorrowful of having committed the act, thoughts that have been developed or behavior that one has adopted, and then asking the Father for forgiveness. Believing that one has been forgiven for whatever their offense may have been, one can then eventually begin displaying an attitude, demeanor and behavior of genuine humility. By faith believe that you have already been forgiven. As the sin is forgiven, the inequity and associated guilt perishes as well.

For one to continue having guilt after having asked for forgiveness, indicates a lack of faith by the individual. By faith we trust in the Father and believe that the confessed sin *is* forgiven; and by so believing and trusting in GOD the Father, we have no need to feel further guilt about any of our confessed and repented actions, thoughts or behaviors whether they are really sinful or not.

Understand that our behavior is often the natural responses to the effects of adapting to our ever changing environment and responding to our inherent instincts of nature. But it is also the result of our GOD given personality combined with those behaviors that stem from our will to survive, and from our attempts to obtain our personal desires. If such things are sin, this too will be revealed to you by the Spirit of GOD dwelling in you, and it will be confirmed by the Spirit of Truth by way of discernment!

This is certainly no ticket to just go get buck wild or do any and everything you want. For if you truly seek the kingdom of GOD, you will become less inclined to do things that are revealed to you as unbecoming of a child of GOD. As you persist in seeking to know and do the will of GOD, many natural animalistic instincts and traits will vanish over time and you will experience less of a desire for things you once pursued. But until then, being human, we will invariably give in to temptation, but we can be certain that we are already forgiven, albeit, we *still* have to *ask* for it. Do you not yet perceive the Father's love for you?

How utterly devastating, disturbing and really saddening it must be for the Hosts of Beings in the universe of Christ Michael's Creation including the enlightened people of this world- to have to endure seeing these deluded humans refer to the Friday before every Easter as 'Good Friday.' In effect celebrating the crucifixion of their beloved Creator with their distorted and perverse perception of spiritual reality and worship; thinking that Christ Michael came to this world as Jesus to be a *sacrifice* for the sins of humankind.

Consider this! Human beings are the lowest form of creature of '*all*' of the Paradise Father's creation in this universe, and there are many beings, personalities and creatures in His Universe. It is indeed arrogant and self righteous beliefs that human beings occupying this world have, thinking that they are the only beings perhaps other than the angels that GOD created in this whole universe. Morontial and spiritual beings must be amused by such insolence and arrogance.

Many professed Christians as yet do not perceive that there are countless universes and many inhabited worlds and many kinds of beings. Still He loves even the lowliest of His creation...human beings; and He loves every single being without being indifferent to any. We are to live our life as we see fit, just with the spiritual enhancement of living it in accordance with the Will of the Father as we perceive it to be.

Get over it! The human race of beings on this world is only *one* in millions of inhabited worlds created by the Order of Michaels; the *Creator Sons* of GOD. To think otherwise is to seriously delimit the power of the Paradise Father and the magnitude of His kingdom in your life.

GOD the Father creates through His Creator Sons and there are many; and these Creator Sons are the Order of Michaels. Each Michael Creator Son of GOD has a number; the number of Michael of Nebadon is 611,121. Christ Michael is now a Master Creator Son, having fulfilled His requirement of being bestowed on and incarnated into beings of His creation. Creator Sons must assume the form of seven beings of Theirs' and the Creative Mother Spirit's creation before They can become the Sovereign ruler of a universe of their creation. The spiritual name of this universe is Nebadon, and elsewhere in the universe, earth is known as Urantia, and Christ Michael's bestowal on earth was His seventh bestowal. He is now the Sovereign GOD of His universe.

It is written in the Scripture: "For GOD so loved the world that He gave His *only begotten Son*, that whosoever believes in Him should not perish but have everlasting life." If you get hungup on the 'only begotten Son' issue, perhaps it would help to realize that Christ Michael is the only begotten Son with the purpose of creating and establishing *His* universe with the goal of bringing every inhabited world in it to the state of Light and Life.

Literally, the Universal Father and the Eternal Son created the Order of Michaels. His Creator Son, Christ Michael of Nebadon *"is* the only begotten son *personalizing this 611,121st universal concept of divinity and infinity."* The Heavenly Father and the Eternal Son created Michael, the incarnate Jesus of Nazareth, to create this universe in which we live and all that there is in it; and He, Michael was the only One created for the express purpose of fulfilling the Father's Will to create this universe which is inhabited by a multitude of beings.

When Jesus, addressing His Apostles stated that there were twelve legions of angels ready to do His bidding, He was even then revealing spiritual reality. Just one legion of angels is enough to decimate the population of this world....hastily and with little effort. But that's just the angels, there were hosts of other beings created by the GOD of this universe that watched in amazement as they witnessed the events leading to and the actual crucifixion of their beloved Master and Creator.

The natural animalistic character traits of human beings is yet to be overcome by the true religion; especially when anything interferes with their exaggerated sense of self power and authority and the monetary profits derived there from. Still His love for His created creatures was so profound that He asked the Paradise Father to "forgive them for they know not what they do" as He was dying of the cross at Golgotha.

Being in the military service one soon comes to realize that there is a hierarchy in place, a chain of command that extends from the lowliest private or person with the least rank, to the generals with the highest rank. Within your unit, your company, battalion and on up to the Commander in Chief (supposedly) which is the President of the United States in our country. The soldier has access to the person who can sufficiently address and resolve their issue(s). There is however a procedure, a system that must be followed in order to proceed to the next higher ranked individual, should the person have a legitimate issue and it was not resolved by the previous person of higher rank.

Well, would it not be reasonable to believe that there is also a hierarchy and a system in place in the spiritual realm to attend to the needs, desires and wants of the children of GOD and to address the affairs, needs and the issues of their worlds? Indeed, there is, and the governments and other organizations of this world are only a shadow of the original, the pattern that has long existed in the spiritual realm.

This government of the Paradise Father is extremely efficient in its coordination, cooperation and organization, emplaced to assist created beings along their journey in the progression to perfection. It takes an infinite capacity of communication between GOD the Father and the Fragment of Himself, His Spirit that dwells within us, to penetrate the language barrier and overcome the thoughts, the acts and other obstacles that keeps us from knowing the Will of the Father.

You have probably heard about the Guardian Angels, and the Archangels in the kingdom of Heaven. It is true! they do exist! The Guardian Angels are called the Seraphic Guardians of Destiny…our destiny. They assist in guiding the Creator Son's created beings into the fulfilling of the Paradise Father's Will and Purpose for our life; while at the same time not interfering with our free will choosing of the path that we decide to take on our journey. They also provide us protection from hurt, harm and danger when we recognize and heed their guidance.

Nevertheless, accidents do sometimes occur, which are random acts or events of which neither we nor the Seraphim overseeing our destiny have control; spontaneous things that we nor they saw coming, and that they didn't perceive as about to happen. Angels, the Seraphim, Cherubim, Sanobim and others are not omniscient. They are not all knowing or all wise and they cannot know the future. They contend with the events happening now. But with foresight, they do with a great deal of accuracy determine the probabilities of what will happen at any given time and in any given situation or circumstance based on our actions, our behavior and our personality. Their actions or nonactions are usually, but not always in accordance with the Will of GOD the Father; such was the case with Lucifer. Lucifer was a Lanonandek Son and a System Sovereign. Lanonandek Sons are also rulers of inhabited planets as Planetary Princes and they do sometimes go astray.

Lucifer, a System Sovereign within the universe of Nebadon, Calagastia the Planetary Prince of Urantia (earth) who is also known as Satan, and Dalagastia, the assistant to the planetary prince, also known as the devil, were Lanonandek Sons with much authority and power. They were coconspirators in Lucifer's rebellion along with many other angels and beings. All of whom are now on a detention world, extinct or they have repented and are being rehabilitated.

Your Seraphic Guardians of Destiny are powerful multifunctioning angels, and they perform various functions but they are not omnipresent, omnipotent, or omniscient. There are two Seraphim who volunteer for the assignment to guard the destiny of each and every one of the Father's beings; His children who are on their journey to Paradise to be as He is...Perfect! One of the Seraphim Angels records everything concerning you. This is the record of your life that will be presented to the Ancients of Days, another Son of GOD who functions in the capacity as Righteous Judges, and who will determine our survival or extinction.

The Ancients of Days, the Creator Sons of GOD and others that come forth from the Paradise Father, they are *Descending* Sons of GOD who is the First Source and Center and GOD the SevenFold. The Paradise Trinity never leave Paradise, but their Created Paradise Sons do. They *descend* from Paradise into the Grand Universe of GOD the Father; into the universes of time and space, each in their own capacity to assist the children of GOD; helping them to learn to live by faith, and helping them to learn and practice godliness and righteousness, and to guide them so that they may survive every step of their long journey to the Isle of Paradise and to perfection.

It should not be difficult for you to believe that ministering spirits from the spiritual realm exists. You have read about them often in Scripture. Eventually, throughout your long spiritual journey to GODlikeness, to perfection, you will encounter many different beings that perform various functions in service to the Heavenly Father and who assist other Descending Sons of GOD; and they too perform services on your behalf in the physical and morontia realms.

They are at work even now attending to you and your fellow brothers and sisters. You will become as one of them...if you're not already; someone performing service to your fellow human beings. You should be one already!

These are only a few of the personalities that exist in the physical, morontia and spiritual realms. There are many others like the cherubim and sanobim, which, according to the Urantia Book are intelligent, efficient and affectionate angels. They are a lower form of angel and they are almost human.

Cherubim and Seraphim you have probably heard about but never really knew their functions and what they really do, but there are other beings called Midway Creatures who are referred to as Midwayers because they are midway between the physical, mortal realm and the morontia realm. These are some phenomenal beings that perform activities that sometimes involve assisting in making spiritual beings become visible in the material world. They themselves are just out of humans' visual range.

It would doubtless be a shock to your religiosity to discover that Adam and Eve were not made from the dust or clay or any other material of this earth; that in fact, they were not made on earth at all; and that they are really Material Sons and Daughters of GOD, and there are many of them. Each are called Adam and Eve and they were transported from Salvington, the capital of the universe of Nebadon in which we live.

The Adams and Eves are biological up lifters. They produce many offspring who mate with the six evolutionary races that usually come to populate inhabited worlds in the universe.

Then the offspring of the children of Adam and Eve, mate with people of evolutionary races biologically up lifting them...or *upgrading* them as you may say in today's parlance.

When you decide to seek for truth rather than fantasy and good feelings, you will be amazed at how plausible, reasonable and sensible the truth that you discover particularly in the Urantia Book truly is; and more so, you will discover that the Spirit of Truth is confirming knowledge that has previously been revealed to you by the Fragment of GOD the Father that dwells within you. This Fragment is called the Thought Adjuster and the Mystery Monitor, and that's what He does. This GOD Fragment adjusts our thoughts as best He can given our proclivities, and He reveals the mysteries of GOD the Father's Will to each and every person that allows Him to perform His purpose in their lives.

Become familiar with some of the multitude of personalities and beings of the Heavenly hosts who are involved in your plan of survival, the plan that GOD the Universal Father has already designed just for you. All of His servants serve as the Father's Will is made known to them. You will no doubt discover that they are particularly helpful in response to requests for objects in which you apply and exercise your faith. These Ministering Spirits get busy bringing to fruition the Will of the Heavenly Father and bringing your faith objects to manifestation.

SUMMARY: THE PRECEPTS OF FAITH AND THE PROCESS OF APPLYING YOUR FAITH

A s with all things in life, how you perceive spiritual reality makes a world of difference in how you behave and react to any given situation or circumstance; and what you believe and act upon is often the difference between prosperity and poverty. Although the precepts are not some magical mystical formula for becoming wealthy, it presents a process by which *faith*, when applied, can bring a measure of prosperity, peace, joy and contentment to your life; regardless of your station in life.

Those sentiments having been expressed, begin building your precepts on these truths as your foundation for applying your faith. Begin at the beginning. Begin with GOD the Universal Father; realizing and acknowledging that He is the *First Source* and *Center*. He is the Originator of all that exists and He is at the center of all that is real, whether it is a spiritual, morontia or physical reality. As Christ Jesus was quoted as saying in Scripture; "But seek first the kingdom of GOD and when once you enter (His Kingdom , therein, all these things will be added unto you."

According to Scripture, "faith is the substance of things *hoped* for, the evidence of things not seen. The major elements or components of faith are *hope, belief* and *trust*. *Hope* for the objects that you need or desire without doubting that you will receive them. Your hope may sometimes waver and your faith waivers right along with it, so endeavor to maintain consistent hope for the object that you are directing your faith toward.

Believe that GOD the Father's Will is that you have the object of your faith. Believe to the point of knowing that you are doing the *work* required (your part to fulfill the conditions necessary to make your faith object come to fruition. Come to understand that "all things work together for good to them that love GOD, to them who are the called according to His purpose." Trust in your Heavenly Father's Love for you, and in His desire that you have the things that will increase your faith so that you will be counted among the righteous.

The Precepts and the Process of faith are inseparable. Believe and receive Christ Jesus of Nazareth as your LORD and SAVIOR:

First, discover who Christ Jesus was as a man of humanity, as the Son of Man; discern as best you can the religion that He practiced, and seek to develop a similar belief system as part of your daily life. This is not to attempt to be like Jesus, but rather to become knowledgeable of the precepts by which He lived, and insert them into your lifestyle; always seeking to know and to do the will of GOD the Father.

Understand that Christ Jesus is the Way; His Way is to live a life free from the bondage of customs, doctrines and traditions that hinders spiritual growth and progress. He is the Truth; His Word is Truth; and His Truth is liberating, setting you free to live your life with only the restrictions imposed by the morals established by GOD His Father, as Christ taught them. Christ Jesus is the Life and no one goes to the Father but by Him. He is our LORD and Savior; accept Him and believe in Him as you would GOD His Father, for Christ Michael *is* the Sovereign GOD and Master Creator Son of His Universe; He who was incarnated in this world as Jesus of Nazareth.

Come to realize that Christ Jesus did not come to earth to be some kind of sacrifice for human beings, to eliminate sins and iniquity. Sacrificing was a system imposed by Moses as a means to pacify the need of the people with superstitious minds who believed that they had to offer something to GOD and even to their idol gods, as a means to appease them and gain their favor and forgiveness. Humankind has always had both, the unwarranted favor of the Father, it's called *'Grace'*; a gift of love bestowed as a token of His goodwill, and we have also had His forgiveness; His infinite capacity to grant pardon for, or remission of an offense or debt (sin). All that has ever been required to obtain an abundance of either is but to ask.

Christ Jesus always said that, "My kingdom is not of this world," though initially many of His Apostles, early disciples and other people didn't take Him seriously when He said it. They were determined to put Him on the throne of King David, and by force if necessary. Their hope was that through the power that He displayed in the miracles He performed, that He would quickly dispose of the Roman occupancy of Israel and bring the Israelites to a state of prominence. Even now people think that Christ Jesus will someday rule from King David's throne, and that the Temple built by King Solomon and destroyed by the Romans will someday be rebuilt. Those were foolish notions then just as they are now, and they give rise to fruitless pursuits.

Christ Jesus of Nazareth sought to disillusion the people of such notions and reveal to them the true Kingdom of GOD; attempting to impart to them that the Kingdom of GOD is within them; and He exhorted them to "Seek *first* the Kingdom of GOD."

Acknowledge GOD the Father:

Acknowledging GOD as your Heavenly Father means coming to realize that you are His faith son or daughter already, and even more so in the making; you are a work in progress! Understand that as a child of GOD you will invariably commit *real* sin and iniquities and make mistakes...some that cost you dearly. But *forgive yourself* of any perceived or real acts of immorality and sin, and recognize, acknowledge and confess any possible disloyal behavior that you have expressed either internally or externally toward the Heavenly Father and ask His forgiveness. Then *know* or wholeheartedly believe that He has already forgiven you. All you need do is to receive His forgiveness. So, receive it and move on! How can you forgive others if you cannot forgive yourself?

When seeking the kingdom of GOD, you also seek His righteousness, for His righteousness is not separate from Him, and you will come to love Him as your Heavenly Father; loving Him with all of your heart, your mind and your strength; depending on Him to know what is best for your life, and trusting Him to lead you to the life that He has already prepared as your destiny.

"In all your ways acknowledge Him and He shall direct your paths." You literally say to the Father, something like; "Heavenly Father I acknowledge you in this situation," or "I acknowledge you with this concern, in the name of Christ Jesus your Son, please guide and direct my path." Or say; "Heavenly Father, I acknowledge that *You* are GOD the First Source and Center, in the name of Christ Jesus your Son, please direct and guide my path. From you, I receive… (*whatever the object of your faith may be* please direct my path in regard to this matter. Nevertheless, not my will, but Your will be done; with the hope that Your will is as mine."

Seek to know and to do the will of GOD the Father concerning your activities and your interactions with your fellow brothers and sisters; which is mainly to "love your neighbor as you love yourself," doing unto others as you would have them do unto you. Learn to love yourself! This is best accomplished when you learn not to compare yourself to other people, but rather, to realize that you are just as much a child of GOD as any other person is, and that he or she is just as much a child of GOD as you are. Accept the truth that GOD the Father loves each of His children the same, unconditionally, and that He has a purpose for your life.

By discovering your gift, your natural abilities and talent, you partially discover the Father's Will and purpose for your life. Though you may have several talents and do several things good, discover what you *naturally* do best; for it will most probably be the Father's gift to you; a gift for you to develop and become proficient and effective in utilizing. Your gift is one of the means by which GOD the Father blesses and graces you that you may prosper and grow, and by which you are to progress in this mortal life.

Request the object of your faith:

The object of your faith can be many different things. It can be spiritual attributes and qualities, and it can also be things that may be of practical use in your everyday life. Whatever *it* is, it must be something that will not cause you or others harm or put either of you in peril or danger or deprive or hinder theirs and your survival in this mortal life, or the life's you will live after this mortal life ends.

You must also realize that the Heavenly Father *does not* encourage undesirable behavior, behavior that is unbecoming of one of His children. Why would He give you something that is not conducive to your spiritual growth and progress? He would not except when it will sometimes later produce the desired effect that He has purposed for you! To do otherwise would be inconsistent with His purpose for your life. With this understanding, make the request known to GOD the Father by faith through prayer and supplication or meditation; asking for the object whatever it may be in the name of Christ Jesus. Again, yielding your will to the Will of the Heavenly Father, trusting with confidence that the actions you perform are those that has been revealed to you by the Spirit of GOD your Thought Adjuster - within you to do; actions that directly or indirectly affect the receiving of your faith object. Believe to the extent of knowing, that the actions you take, the works that you do are in response to the leading of the Seraphic Guardians of Destiny; that your actions are in accordance with the Will of GOD as revealed by the Spirit of GOD who dwells within you, and by the Holy Spirit who imparts the necessary knowledge you will require. They will direct you to the doors of opportunity that will open up to you for your experience of faith object manifestation.

Be aware that when you request something from your Heavenly Father, if it is His Will that you receive your requested object, you will almost immediately begin to experience events or situations that come upon you like a sudden storm; things which you will undoubtedly perceive as troubles, trials, or unpleasant phenomenon that make your life difficult for a *season.*

You must be undaunted by these things. You must endure them and persevere; for in doing so, you acquire needed qualities that enhances your faith and cause you to appreciate the object of your need or desire all the more.

Learn to recognize the revelations and the leading and guiding of the Ministering Spirits and the Spiritual Personalities of the Heavenly hosts. They are intimately involved in your progression to perfection. Believing that the Father employs various Beings to assist in answering your prayers and requests is key to having the assurance and confidence that you will receive the object of your faith. Yes, you may *wonder* or *speculate* about it, but never doubt that the Will of the Father will prevail, and that you will receive the object of your faith in due time, in due season.

Understand that the *due season* may not be in this lifetime. There are prayer requests that are too complex and complicated for you to receive in this mortal life. These will be more accessible and readily received in the morontia life; the life that all surviving humans ascend to after death from this mortal life; a life that is more sensitive to revelations of the Heavenly Father by way of the Fragment of His Spirit dwelling within you. But in the morontia life you are still not yet pure spirit. Some of your prayer requests will only be answered when you attain eternal life, when you are pure spirit.

Recognize your Seasons:

Your life is one long series of events and experiences. However, the events and experiences are not just random acts that have no meaning. There have been times in your life when you have prospered and there are times when you have succumbed to deprivation. There have been times when you have perceived a special closeness with GOD the Father and with Christ Jesus...They are as One! And there are times when you have felt neglected or abandoned and all alone.

In times of deprivation, when feelings of abandonment overwhelm you and in times of sadness, sickness, grief and other conditions that may befall you, there are lessons to be learned from your Ministering Spirits. Try to listen with your heart (in stillness) to discover how the Heavenly Father is preparing you to receive, just as a gardener may prepare soil for a garden.

Reflect back over your life's experiences, being careful to *observe* the *seasons* that have occurred and recurred at different times in your life. Understand that '*all*' of life is a learning process, but there are particular times when the Heavenly Father 'makes' you to lie down in green pastures so that He can restore your soul. The Father has special instructions for you; instructions that will enable you to overcome the circumstance or situation in which you find yourself. He has particular tasks for you to accomplish and you will need strength, both physical and spiritual strength to meet the challenges that lie just ahead; especially when the tasks involve engaging or interacting with your fellow brothers and sisters and people of authority with love and respect, imparting spiritual reality and truth to them.

During the cultivating season prepare the soil of your heart by receiving the knowledge being revealed to you by the Spirit of GOD and the Holy Spirit within. Sharpen the skills, the talents and gifts that GOD the Father has bestowed within your personality; and then in the *sowing season* employ them, putting them to work; sow the seeds which will invariably lead to your prosperity; use your gifts and talents in the service of GOD the Father, and in service to humankind, and to bring prosperity to yourself as well.

In the *season of harvest* you *will* reap prosperity. Understand that prosperity comes in a variety of forms, not just through the possession of wealth; there is spiritual prosperity that comes in the form of the Fruit of the Spirit, and in the form of knowledge, wisdom and understanding. You may also receive physical prosperity in the form of good health and well being, notwithstanding the natural physical diseases, illnesses and other issues and maladies that are common to mankind.

But you may prosper materially as well; this comes in the form of money and any other material things that are GOD the Father's Will for you to have.

Be conscious of the fact, the truth that just as seasons naturally and gradually change from one to the other, that the manifestation of your faith object doesn't happen instantaneously. Miracles do happen all the time but there is an overlap of the seasons. Seasons don't usually come to an abrupt halt before the next one begins. So be prepared to endure and accomplish the tasks to be performed in and through each season of your life. Wait for the *doors of opportunity* to open so that you may begin to *experience* and perform the *process* that brings you *your* prosperity.

Once you receive your prosperity, when the object of your faith has come to fruition and has been made manifest, it is then time to enjoy the fruit of your labor in the *season of the feast.* Invite family, friends and strangers to partake in the festivities and celebrate the prosperity that your Heavenly Father has blessed and graced you with.

Humble yourself and Ask, Seek and Knock:

How often do people in their *foolish* pride fail to ask for something that they may desperately need or that they simply desire to have? They find it degrading and humiliating to their ego, and *that* would offend their sensibilities to ask for help. But that is exactly what the Heavenly Father requires of His Children; to ask Him for whatever we need or desire.

Yes, pride can be a good thing! The kind of pride that elicits self esteem, and causes people to maintain socially and religiously acceptable appearances, attitudes and behaviors; it is a kind of pride that incites self-motivation to accomplish amazing things. Confidence in one's abilities is an admirable quality and trait when that confidence is not obscured by tunnel vision, and when it is not self defeating, self limiting...or totally self serving.

Ask your Heavenly Father for what you need or desire. He is the First Source and Center, everything else is resources. *Seek* Truth, Beauty, and Goodness; for these are the things that produce spirit value. This is the method by which you send up your timber...so to speak! Knock on the door, any door...literally! If you don't do the smallest and most easy tasks, how inclined will you be to do the larger and more difficult ones?

Be vigilant! Be observant and astute enough to recognize when opportunity presents itself; and be persistent in your endeavor to employ your faith. Your methods may vary, but maintain persistence in pursuing the object of your faith. Keep asking, keep seeking and keep knocking until you receive the object of your faith; always giving thanks to GOD in advance, as this portrays an attitude of expectancy in *hope* of your receiving the object that you asked from the Father.

In due time and in *your* due season, you will receive the object of your faith; and as you continue to apply and exercise your faith, the stronger your faith becomes, and you will have ample opportunities to apply and exercise your faith in some manner, directing it toward some object. You need not worry or be concerned about doing something right or wrong because *all* things work together for the good of them that love GOD, to them who are called according to His purpose. Try to make His purpose your purpose, and His Will your will, because, while your will and purpose for your life may be good, the Heavenly Father's Will and Purpose for your life is infinitely better. Live your life and prosper in the Kingdom of your Heavenly Father!

COMMENTS, QUOTES AND REFERENCES:

Prologue

1 **John 1:11-13 (KJV)** (11) He came unto his own, and his own received him not.

    (12)   But as many as received him, to them gave he power to become the sons of GOD, even to them that believe on his name:

    (13)   Which were born, not of blood, nor of the will of the flesh, nor of the will of man, but of GOD.

2 **(see Matthew 12:27-28, Luke 11:14-20)**

3 **Revelation 12:7-8 (NKJV)**

    (7)   And war broke out in heaven: Michael and his angels fought with the dragon; and the dragon and his angels fought,

    (8)   but they did not prevail, nor was a place found for them in heaven any longer.

Daniel 12:1 (KJV)

    (1)   And at that time shall Michael stand up, the great prince which standeth for the children of thy people: and there shall be a time of trouble, such as never was since there was a nation even to that same time: and at that time thy people shall be delivered, every one that shall be found written in the book.

Perceptions of GOD the Father

John 10:10 (KJV)

(10)   The thief cometh not, but for to steal, and to
kill, and to destroy: I am come that they might
have life, and that they might have it more
abundantly.

(Quote from the Urantia Book: pg. 2017; Paper 188:
Section   4,   paragraph   8;   and   online:
http://www.urantia.org/urantiabookstandardized/paper-188-
timetomb)

Luke 10:21-22 (KJV)

(21)   In that hour Jesus rejoiced in spirit, and said,
I thank thee, O Father, Lord of heaven and
earth, that thou hast hid these things from the
wise and prudent, and hast revealed them
unto babes: even so, Father; for so it seemed
good in thy sight.

(22)   All things are delivered to me of my Father:
and no man knoweth who the Son is, but the
Father; and who the Father is, but the Son,
and he to whom the Son will reveal him.

John 14:6-11 (KJV)

(6)   Jesus saith unto him, I am the way, the truth, and the life:
no man cometh unto the Father, but by me.

(7)   If ye had known me, ye should have known my Father
also: and from henceforth ye know him, and have seen
him.

(8)   Philip saith unto him, Lord, shew us the Father, and it sufficeth us.

(9)   Jesus saith unto him, "Have I been so long time with you, and yet hast thou not known me, Philip? he that hath seen me hath seen the Father; and how sayest thou then, Shew us the Father?

(10)   Believest thou not that I am in the Father, and the Father in me? the words that I speak unto you I speak not of myself: but the Father that dwelleth in me, he doeth the works.

(11)   Believe me that I am in the Father, and the Father in me: or else believe me for the very works' sake.

John 14:12-14 (KJV)

(12)   Verily, verily, I say unto you, He that believeth on me, the works that I do shall he do also; and greater works than these shall he do; because I go unto my Father.

(13)   And whatsoever ye shall ask in my name, that will I do, that the Father may be glorified in the Son.

(14)   If ye shall ask any thing in my name, I will do it.

Matthew 5:43-47 (KJV)

(43)   Ye have heard that it hath been said, Thou shalt love thy neighbor, and hate thine enemy.

(44)   But I say unto you, Love your enemies, bless them that curse you, do good to them that hate you, and pray for them which despitefully use you, and persecute you;

(45)   That ye may be the children of your Father which is in heaven: for he maketh his sun to rise on the evil and on the good, and sendeth rain on the just and on the unjust.

(46)   For if ye love them which love you, what reward have ye? do not even the publicans the same?

(47)   And if ye salute your brethren only, what do ye more than others? do not even the publicans so?

Thessalonians 5:18-19 (KJV)

(18)   In every thing give thanks: for this is the His Will in Christ Jesus concerning you.

(19)   Quench not the Spirit.

Matthew 5:48 (KJV)

(48)   Be ye therefore perfect, even as your Father which is in heaven is perfect.

Luke 10:21-22 (NKJV)

(21)   In that hour Jesus rejoiced in the Spirit and said, "I thank You, Father, Lord of heaven and earth, that You have hidden these things from the wise and prudent and revealed them to babes. Even so, Father, for so it seemed good in Your sight.

(22)   All things have been delivered to Me by My Father, and no one knows who the Son is except the Father, and who the Father is except the Son, and the one to whom the Son wills to reveal Him."

Potential made Actual by Faith

No   references...

The Abundant Life

John 10:10 (KJV)

(10) The thief cometh not, but for to steal, and to kill, and to destroy: I am come that they might have life, and that they might have it more abundantly.

Mark 7:5-13 (KJV)

(5) Then the Pharisees and scribes asked him, Why walk not thy disciples according to the tradition of the elders, but eat bread with unwashen hands?

(6) He answered and said unto them, Well hath Esaias prophesied of you hypocrites, as it is written, This people honoureth me with their lips, but their heart is far from me.

(5) Howbeit in vain do they worship me, teaching for doctrines the commandments of men.

(5) For laying aside the commandment of GOD, ye hold the tradition of men, as the washing of pots and cups: and many other such like things ye do.

(6) And he said unto them, Full well ye reject the commandment of GOD, that ye may keep your own tradition.

(7) For Moses said, Honour thy Father and thy mother; and, Whoso curseth Father or mother, let him die the death:

(11) But ye say, If a man shall say to his Father or mother, It is Corban, that is to say, a gift, by whatsoever thou mightest be profited by me; he shall be free.

(12) And ye suffer him no more to do ought for his Father or his mother;

(13) Making the word of GOD of none effect through your tradition, which ye have delivered: and many such like things do ye.

Daniel 7:13-14 (KJV)

(13)   I saw in the night visions, and, behold, one like the Son of man came with the clouds of heaven, and came to the Ancient of days, and they brought him near before him.

(14)   And there was given him dominion, and glory, and a kingdom, that all people, nations, and languages, should serve him: his dominion is an everlasting dominion, which shall not pass away, and his kingdom that which shall not be destroyed.

Daniel 7:21-22 (KJV)

(21)   I beheld, and the same horn made war with the saints, and prevailed against them;

(22)   Until the Ancient of days came, and judgment was given to the saints of the most High; and the time came that the saints possessed the kingdom.

Philippians 4:19 (KJV)

(19)   But my GOD shall supply all your need according to his riches in glory by Christ Jesus.

The Divine You and the Human You
Matthew 17:20 (KJV)

(20)   And Jesus said unto them, Because of your unbelief: for verily I say unto you, If ye have faith as a grain of mustard seed, ye shall say unto this mountain, Remove hence to yonder place; and it shall remove; and nothing shall be impossible unto you.

Matthew 25:14-29 (KJV)

(14)   For the kingdom of heaven is as a man travelling into a far country, who called his own servants, and delivered unto them his goods.

(15)   And unto one he gave five talents, to another two, and to another one; to every man according to his several ability; and straightway took his journey.

(16)   Then he that had received the five talents went and traded with the same, and made them other five talents.

(17)   And likewise he that had received two, he also gained other two.

(18)   But he that had received one went and digged in the earth, and hid his lord's money.

(19)   After a long time the lord of those servants cometh, and reckoneth with them.

(20)   And so he that had received five talents came and brought other five talents, saying, Lord, thou deliveredst unto me five talents: behold, I have gained beside them five talents more.

(21)   His lord said unto him, Well done, thou good and faithful servant: thou hast been faithful over a few things, I will make thee ruler over many things: enter thou into the joy of thy lord.

(14)   He also that had received two talents came and said, Lord, thou deliveredst unto me two talents: behold, I have gained two other talents beside them.

(15)   His lord said unto him, Well done, good and faithful servant; thou hast been faithful over a few things, I will make thee ruler over many things: enter thou into the joy of thy lord.

(16)   Then he which had received the one talent came and said, Lord, I knew thee that thou art an hard man, reaping where thou hast not sown, and gathering where thou hast not strawed:

(17)   And I was afraid, and went and hid thy talent in the earth: lo, there thou hast that is thine.

(18)   His lord answered and said unto him, Thou wicked and slothful servant, thou knewest that I reap where I sowed not, and gather where I have not strawed:

(19)   Thou oughtest therefore to have put my money to the exchangers, and then at my coming I should have received mine own with usury.

(20)   Take therefore the talent from him, and give it unto him which hath ten talents.

(21)   For unto every one that hath shall be given, and he shall have abundance: but from him that hath not shall be taken away even that which he hath. 3

(See: Luke   10:27   NKJV)
The Urantia Book is a revelation of truth about GOD the Father, the Grand Universe and the Celestial Hosts who occupy it, and the life and teachings of Christ Jesus. The Urantia Book explains who He was before His incarnation on earth (Urantia) and who He is now. It is a compilation of information, truth, as I have discerned it to be, written by various personalities of the Heavenly hosts of beings in the spiritual realm; Beings who are involved with the spiritual progress of the human race of beings on this sphere, this planet in their efforts to literally bring the kingdom of GOD to every person occupying space in time. This book reveals the true history, the creation of the Universe, earth and human beings. (See: The Urantia Book; http:// urantiabook.   org/newbook/)

Confirmation of the Truth...

From the book; The Center Within Lessons from the Heart of the Urantia Revelation by Fred Harris and Byron Belitsos: pg. 270, glossary under Spirit of Truth; Copyright 1998 by Mind, Body & Spirit.

John 14:4-6 (KJV)

(4)   And whither I go ye know, and the way ye know.

(5)   Thomas saith unto him, Lord, we know not whither thougoest; and how can we know the way?

(6)   Jesus saith unto him, I am the way, the truth, and the   life: no man cometh unto the Father, but by me.

(An excerpt from the Urantia Book: The teachings of Jesus; His second discourse on the true religion.)

"You must cease to seek for the word of GOD only on the pages of the olden records of theologic authority. Those who are born of the spirit of GOD shall henceforth discern the word of GOD regardless of whence it appears to take origin. Divine truth must not be discounted because the channel of its bestowal is apparently human. Many of your brethren have minds which accept the theory of GOD while they spiritually fail to realize the presence of GOD. And that is just the reason why I have so often taught you that the kingdom of heaven can best be realized by acquiring the spiritual attitude of a sincere child. It is not the mental immaturity of the child that I commend to you but rather the spiritual simplicity of such an easybelieving and fullytrusting little one.

It is not so important that you should know about the fact of GOD as that you should increasingly grow in the ability to feel the presence of GOD."http://urantiabook.org/newbook/papers/p155.htm

(see:TheUrantiaBook;http://www.urantia.org/en urantiabookstandardizedpaper-1universalfather)

Proverbs 4:4-9 (KJV)

(4)   He taught me also, and said unto me, Let thine heart retain my words: keep my commandments, and live.

(5)   Get wisdom, get understanding: forget it not; neither decline from the words of my mouth.

(6)   Forsake her not, and she shall preserve thee: love her, and she shall keep thee.

(7)   Wisdom is the principal thing; therefore get wisdom: and with all thy getting get understanding.

(8)   Exalt her, and she shall promote thee: she shall bring thee to honour, when thou dost embrace her.

(9)   She shall give to thine head an ornament of grace: crown of glory shall she deliver to thee.

Matthew 6:31-33 (KJV)

(31)   Therefore take no thought, saying, What shall we eat? or, What shall we drink? or, Wherewithal shall we be clothed?

(32)   (For after all these things do the Gentiles seek:) for your Heavenly Father knows that you have need of all these things.

(33)   But seek ye first the kingdom of GOD, and his righteousness; and all these things shall be added unto you.

Faith and how it is Applied

Matthew 17:20 (KJV)

(20)   And Jesus said unto them, Because of your unbelief: for verily I say unto you, If ye have faith as a grain of mustard seed, ye shall say unto this mountain, Remove hence to yonder place; and it shall remove; and nothing shall be impossible unto you.

Timothy 3:1-7 (NKJV)

(1)   But know this, that in the last days perilous times will come:

(2)   For men will be lovers of themselves, lovers of money, boasters, proud, blasphemers, disobedient to parents, unthankful, unholy,

(3)   unloving, unforgiving, slanderers, without self- control, brutal, despisers of good,

(4)   traitors, headstrong, haughty, lovers of pleasure rather than lovers of GOD,

(5)   having a form of godliness but denying its power. And from such people turn away!

(6)   For of this sort are those who creep into households and make captives of gullible women loaded down with sins, led away by various lusts,

(7)   always learning and never able to come to the knowledge of the truth.

Hebrews 11:1-3 (KJV)

(1)   Now faith is the substance of things hoped for, the evidence of things not seen.

(2)   For by it the elders obtained a good report.

(3)   Through faith we understand that the worlds were framed by the word of GOD, so that things which are seen were not made of things which do appear.

(See Webster's New World Dictionary of the American Language-College Edition; copyright 1966; pg. 1454)

Romans 8:28 (KJV)

(28)   And we know that all things work together for good to them that love GOD, to them who are the called according to his purpose.

Romans 8:28 (KJV)

(5)   Who serve unto the example and shadow of Heavenly things, as Moses was admonished of GOD when he was about to make the tabernacle: for, See, saith he, that thou make all things according to the pattern shewed to thee in the mount.

John 1:10-13 (KJV)

(10)   He was in the world, and the world was made by him, and the world knew him not.

(11)   He came unto his own, and his own received him not.

(12)   But as many as received him, to them gave he power to become the sons of GOD, even to them that believe on his name:

(13)   Which were born, not of blood, nor of the will of the flesh, nor of the will of man, but of GOD.

Life's Seasons

Ecclesiastes 3:1-2 (KJV)

(1)   For everything there is a season, and a time for every purpose under heaven:

(2)   a time to be born, and a time to die; a time to plant, and a time to pluck up that which is planted;

See Romans 8:28 (KJV)

Thessalonians 5:16-18 (KJV)

(16)   Rejoice evermore.

(17)   Pray without ceasing.

(18)   In everything give thanks: for this is the will of GOD in Christ Jesus concerning you.

Luke 11:9 (KJV)

(9) And I say unto you, Ask, and it shall be given you; seek, and ye shall find; knock, and it shall be opened unto you.

John 8:31-32 (KJV)

(31)   Then said Jesus to those Jews which believed on him, If ye (you) continue in my word, then are ye my disciples indeed;

(32)   And ye shall know the truth, and the truth shall make you free.

John 1:12-13 (KJV)

(12)   But as many as received him, to them gave he power to become the sons of GOD, even to them that believe on his name:

(13)   Which were born, not of blood, nor of the will of the flesh, nor of the will of man, but of GOD.

Opening Doors

See Luke 11:9-10 (KJV)

John 10:9-11 (KJV)

(9)   I am the door: by me if any man enter in, he shall be saved, and shall go in and out, and find pasture.

(10)   The thief cometh not, but for to steal, and to kill, and to destroy: I am come that they might have life, and that they might have it more abundantly.

(9)   I am the good shepherd: the good shepherd giveth his life for the sheep.

Psalms 23:1-6 (KJV)

(1)   The LORD is my shepherd; I shall not want.

(2)   He maketh me to lie down in green pastures: he leadeth me beside the still waters.

(3)   He restoreth my soul: he leadeth me in the paths of righteousness for his name's sake.

(4)   Yea, though I walk through the valley of the shadow of death, I will fear no evil: for thou art with me; thy rod and thy staff they comfort me.

(5)   Thou preparest a table before me in the presence of mine enemies: thou anointest my head with oil; my cup runneth over.

(6)   Surely goodness and mercy shall follow me all the days of my life: and I will dwell in the house of the LORD for ever.

Recognizing and receiving the object of your Faith

John 3:16 (KJV)

(16)   For GOD so loved the world, that he gave his only begotten Son, that whosoever believeth in him should not perish, but have everlasting life.

Matthew 18:21-22 (KJV)

(21)   Then came Peter to him, and said, Lord, how oft shall my brother sin against me, and I forgive him? till seven times?

(22)   Jesus saith unto him, I say not unto thee, Until seven times: but, Until seventy times seven.

Luke 11:9-10 (KJV)

(9)   And I say unto you, Ask, and it shall be given you; seek, and ye shall find; knock, and it shall be opened unto you.

(10)   For every one that asketh receiveth; and he that seeketh findeth; and to him that knocketh it shall be opened.

John 12:8 (KJV)

(8)   For the poor always ye have with you; but me ye have not always.

Contrast between Religion and Spirituality...
(Quote from the Urantia Book: pg. 2082; Paper 195: Section 9, and from the book; The Center Within Lessons from the Heart of the Urantia Revelation by Fred Harris and Byron Belitsos:
Copyright 1998 by Mind, Body & Spirit)

(Quote from the Urantia Book: pg. 1782; Paper 160: Section 5, paragraph-13)

The consciousness of the impulse to be like GOD is not true religion. The feelings of the emotion to worship GOD are not true religion. The knowledge of the conviction to forsake self and serve GOD is not true religion. The wisdom of the reasoning that this religion is the best of all is not religion as a personal and spiritual experience. True religion has reference to destiny and reality of attainment as well as to the reality and idealism of that which is wholeheartedly faithaccepted. And all of this must be made personal to us by the revelation of the Spirit of Truth.

(Quote from the Urantia Book: pg. 1781; Paper 160: Section 5, paragraph-5)

The social characteristics of a true religion consist in the fact that it invariably seeks to convert the individual and to transform the world. Religion implies the existence of undiscovered ideals which far transcend the known standards of ethics and morality embodied in even the highest social usages of the most mature institutions of civilization. Religion reaches out for undiscovered ideals, unexplored realities, superhuman values, divine wisdom, and true spirit attainment. True religion does all of this; all other beliefs are not worthy of the name. You cannot have a genuine spiritual religion without the supreme and supernal ideal of an eternal GOD. A religion without this GOD is an invention of man, a human institution of lifeless intellectual beliefs and meaningless emotional ceremonies. A religion might claim as the object of its devotion a great ideal. But such ideals of unreality are not attainable; such a concept is illusionary. The only ideals susceptible of human attainment are the divine realities of the infinite values resident in the spiritual fact of the eternal GOD.

(An excerpt from the Urantia Book: The Life and Teachings of Jesus; page 1729; Paper 155; section 5, paragraphs 5).(See:http://urantiabook.org/newbook/papers/p155.htm)

John 1:1-4 (KJV)

(1)   In the beginning was the Word, and the Word was with GOD, and the Word was GOD.

(2)   The same was in the beginning with GOD.

(3)   All things were made by him; and without him was not anything made that was made.

(4)   In him was life; and the life was the light of men. True religion the religion of revelation. The revelation of supernatural values, a partial insight into eternal realities, a glimpse of the goodness and beauty of the infinite character of the Father in heaven the religion of the spirit as demonstrated in human experience.

Until the races become highly intelligent and more fully civilized, there will persist many of those childlike and superstitious ceremonies which are so characteristic of the evolutionary religious practices of primitive and backward peoples. Until the human race progresses to the level of a higher and more general recognition of the realities of spiritual experience, large numbers of men and women will continue to show a personal preference for those religions of authority which require only intellectual assent, in contrast to the religion of the spirit, which entails active participation of mind and soul in the faith adventure of grappling with the rigorous realities of progressive human experience.

The acceptance of the traditional religions of authority presents the easy way out for man's urge to seek satisfaction for the longings of his spiritual nature. The settled, crystallized, and established religions of authority afford a ready refuge to which the distracted and distraught soul of man may flee when harassed by fear and tormented by uncertainty. Such a religion requires of its devotees, as the price to be paid for its satisfactions and assurances, only a passive and purely intellectual assent.

(An excerpt from the Urantia Book: The Life and Teachings of Jesus; page 1729; Paper 155; section 5, paragraphs 5, 8 & 9).

And for a long time there will live on earth those timid, fearful, and hesitant individuals who will prefer thus to secure their religious consolations, even though, in so casting their lot with the religions of authority, they compromise the sovereignty of personality, debase the dignity of self-respect, and utterly surrender the right to participate in that most thrilling and inspiring of all possible human experiences: the personal quest for truth, the exhilaration of facing the perils of intellectual discovery, the determination to explore the realities of personal religious experience, the supreme satisfaction of experiencing the personal triumph of the actual realization of the victory of spiritual faith over intellectual doubt as it is honestly won in the supreme adventure of all human existence man seeking GOD, for himself and as himself, and finding him.

The religion of the spirit means effort, struggle, conflict, faith, determination, love, loyalty, and progress. The religion of the mind the theology of authority requires little or none of these exertions from its formal believers. Tradition is a safe refuge and an easy path for those fearful and halfhearted souls who instinctively shun the spirit struggles and mental uncertainties associated with those faith voyages of daring adventure out upon the high seas of unexplored truth in search for the farther shores of spiritual realities as they may be discovered by the progressive human mind and experienced by the evolving human soul.

(An excerpt from the Urantia Book: The Life and Teachings of Jesus; The discourse on True Religion, page 1729; Paper 155; section 5, paragraphs 10 & 11.)

(An excerpt from the Urantia Book; paper 168; section 4; pages 1848 & 1849; paragraphs 2, 3, 4 & 5. See also: http:// urantiabook.org/newbook/papers/p168.htm)

The context: "The apostles were much stirred up in their minds and spent considerable time discussing their recent experiences as they were related to prayer and its answering. They all recalled Jesus' statement to the Bethany messenger at Philadelphia, when he said plainly, "This sickness is not really to the death." And yet, in spite of this promise, Lazarus actually died. All that day, again and again, they reverted to the discussion of this question of the answer to prayer."

"Jesus' answers to their many questions may be summarized as follows:"

1. "Prayer is an expression of the finite mind in an effort to approach the Infinite. The making of a prayer must, therefore, be limited by the knowledge, wisdom, and attributes of the finite; likewise must the answer be conditioned by the vision, aims, ideals, and prerogatives of the Infinite. There never can be observed an unbroken continuity of material phenomena between the making of a prayer and the reception of the full spiritual answer thereto."

2. "When a prayer is apparently unanswered, the delay often betokens a better answer, although one which is for some good reason greatly delayed. When Jesus said that Lazarus's sickness was really not to the death, he had already been dead eleven hours. No sincere prayer is denied an answer except when the superior viewpoint of the spiritual world has devised a better answer, an answer which meets the petition of the spirit of man as contrasted with the prayer of the mere mind of man."

(An excerpt from the Urantia Book; paper 168; section 4; pages 1848 & 1849. See also: http://urantiabook.org/newbook/papers p168.htm)

3. "The prayers of time, when indited by the spirit and expressed in faith, are often so vast and all encompassing that they can be answered only in eternity; the finite petition is sometimes so fraught with the grasp of the Infinite that the answer must long be postponed to await the creation of adequate capacity for receptivity; the prayer of faith may be so all-embracing that the answer can be received only on Paradise."

4. "The answers to the prayer of the mortal mind are often of such a nature that they can be received and recognized only after that same praying mind has attained the immortal state. The prayer of the material being can many times be answered only when such an individual has progressed to the spirit level."

5. "The prayer of a GOD knowing person may be so distorted by ignorance and so deformed by superstition that the answer there to would be highly undesirable. Then must the intervening spirit beings so translate such a prayer that, when the answer arrives, the petitioner wholly fails to recognize it as the answer to his prayer."

6. "All true prayers are addressed to spiritual beings, and all such petitions must be answered in spiritual terms, and all such answers must consist in spiritual realities. Spirit beings cannot bestow material answers to the spirit petitions of even material beings. Material beings can pray effectively only when they "pray in the spirit.""

7. "No prayer can hope for an answer unless it is born of the spirit and nurtured by faith. Your sincere faith implies that you have in advance virtually granted your prayer hearers the full right to answer your petitions in accordance with that supreme wisdom and that divine love which your faith depicts as always actuating those beings to whom you pray."

8. "The child is always within his rights when he presumes to petition the parent; and the parent is always within his parental obligations to the immature child when his superior wisdom dictates that the answer to the child's prayer be delayed, modified, segregated, transcended, or postponed to another stage of spiritual ascension."

9. "Do not hesitate to pray the prayers of spirit longing; doubt not that you shall receive the answer to your petitions. These answers will be on deposit, awaiting your achievement of those future spiritual levels of actual cosmic attainment, on this world or on others, whereon it will become possible for you to recognize and appropriate the long waiting answers to your earlier but ill-timed petitions."

10. "All genuine spirit born petitions are certain of an answer. Ask and you shall receive. But you should remember that you are progressive creatures of time and space; therefore must you constantly reckon with the time space factor in the experience of your personal reception of the full answers to your manifold prayers and petitions."

Romans 8:26-27 (NKJV)

(26)   Likewise the Spirit also helps in our weaknesses. For we do not know what we should pray for as we ought, but the Spirit Himself makes intercession for us with groanings which cannot be uttered.

(27)   Now He who searches the hearts knows what the mind of the Spirit is, because He makes intercession for the saints according to the Will of GOD.

Living Your Life by Faith

Galatians 5:21-25 (NKJV)

Romans 8:26-27 (NKJV)

(26)   Likewise the Spirit also helps in our weaknesses. For we do not know what we should pray for as we ought, but the Spirit Himself makes intercession for us with groanings which cannot be uttered.

(27)   Now He who searches the hearts knows what the mind of the Spirit is, because He makes intercession for the saints according to the Will of GOD.

Living Your Life by Faith
Galatians 5:21-25 (NKJV)

(22)   But the fruit of the Spirit is love, joy, peace longsuffering, kindness, goodness, faithfulness,

(23)   gentleness, self control. Against such there is no law.

(24)   And those who are Christ's have crucified the flesh with its passions and desires.

25)   If we live in the Spirit, let us also walk in the Spirit.

Mark 12:30-31 (NKJV)

(30)   And you shall love the Lord your GOD with all your heart, with all your soul, with all your mind, and with all your strength.' This is the first commandment.

(31)   And the second, like it, is this: 'You shall love your neighbor as yourself.' There is no other commandment greater than these."

Matthew 7:4-5 (KJV)

(4)   Or how wilt thou say to thy brother, Let me pull out the mote out of thine eye; and, behold, a beam is in thine own eye?

(5)   Thou hypocrite, first cast out the beam out of thine own eye; and then shalt thou see clearly to cast out the mote out of thy brother's eye.

Luke 6:37-38 (KJV)

(37) Judge not, and ye shall not be judged: condemn not, and ye shall not be condemned: forgive, and ye shall be forgiven:

(38) Give, and it shall be given unto you; good measure, pressed down, and shaken together, and running over, shall men give into your bosom. For with the same measure that ye mete withal it shall be measured to you again.

Hebrews 12:6-11 (NKJV)

(6) For whom the Lord loves He chastens, and scourges every son whom He receives."

(7) If you endure chastening, GOD deals with you as with sons; for what son is there whom a Father does not chasten?

(8) But if you are without chastening, of which all have become partakers, then you are illegitimate and not sons.

(9) Furthermore, we have had human Fathers who corrected us, and we paid them respect. Shall we not much more readily be in subjection to the Father of spirits and live?

For they indeed for a few days chastened us as seemed best to them, but He for our profit, that we may be partakers of His holiness. Now no chastening seems to be joyful for the present, but painful; nevertheless, afterward it yields the peaceable fruit of righteousness to those who have been trained by it.

Romans 8:27-28 (KJV)

(27) And he that searcheth the hearts knoweth what is the mind of the Spirit, because he maketh intercession for the saints according to the His Will.

(28) And we know that all things work together for good to them that love GOD, to them who are the called according to his purpose.

Philippians 4:18-19 (NASB77)

(18)   But I have received everything in full, and have an abun- dance; I am amply supplied, having received from Epaphroditus what you have sent, a fragrant aroma, an acceptable sacrifice, well pleasing to GOD.

(19)   And my GOD shall supply all your needs according to His riches in glory in Christ Jesus.

Hebrews 11:1-3 (KJV)

(1)   Now faith is the substance of things hoped for, the evidence of things not seen.   (2) For by it the elders obtained a good report.

(2)   For by it the elders obtained a good report.

(3)   Through faith we understand that the worlds were framed by the word of GOD, so that things which are seen were not made of things which do appear.
(See the UrantiaBookhttp://www.urantia.org/en/urantia-book/read)

Thessalonians 5:16-19 (KJV)

(16)   Rejoice evermore.

(17)   Pray without ceasing.

(18)   In everything give thanks: for this is the His Will in Christ Jesus concerning you.

(19)   Quench not the Spirit.

The Inspired Word of GOD

Melchizedek is mentioned numerous times in Bible Scripture, but He is only referred to as a High Priest, see: Genesis 14:18, Psalms 110:4₂ , Hebrews 5:6 & 10, Hebrews 6:20, and Hebrews 7th chapter The Ancients of Days is mentioned mostly in the book of Daniel. Daniel 7:22 indicates that the Ancients of Days is associated with judging the saints of GOD, and then later in time the saints possessed the Kingdom of Heaven.

Genesis 1:26 (KJV)

(26)   And GOD said, Let us make man in our image, after our likeness: and let them have dominion over the fish of the sea, and over the fowl of the air, and over the cattle, and over all the earth, and over every creeping thing that creepeth upon the earth.

Genesis 2:4-7 (KJV)

(4)   These are the generations of the heavens and of the earth when they were created, in the day that the LORD GOD made the earth and the heavens,

(5)   And every plant of the field before it was in the earth, and every herb of the field before it grew: for the LORD GOD had not caused it to rain upon the earth, and there was not a man to till the ground.

(6)   But there went up a mist from the earth, and watered the whole face of the ground.

(7)   And the LORD GOD formed man of the dust of the ground, and breathed into his nostrils the breath of life; and man became a living soul.

Genesis 4:13-15 (KJV)

(13)   And Cain said unto the LORD, My punishment is greater than I can bear.

(14)   Behold, thou hast driven me out this day from the face of the earth; and from thy face shall I be hid; and I shall be a fugitive and a vagabond in the earth; and it shall come to pass, that every one that findeth me shall slay me.

(15)   And the LORD said unto him, Therefore whosoever slayeth Cain, vengeance shall be taken on him sevenfold. And the LORD set a mark upon Cain, lest any finding him should kill him.

See the Urantia Book; Paper 74; Adam and Eve, page 828;   http://www.urantia.org/urantiabook-standardized/paper-74 adamandeve6

(See Hebrews 5:6,5:10, 6:20 & 7:1, 7:10 & 7:11)

Christians and Jesusonians Defined

(See Acts 22:25-30 KJV)

(SeeMatthew16:17-18 KJV)

(See Matthew 7:7 KJV)

(See John 8:31-32)

The Evolutionary Truth of the Creation

(An excerpt from the Urantia Book; see:http://www.urantia. org/urantia-book-standardized/paper-147interludevisitjerusalem;   section-7,   paragraph-3)   2 (See: The Urantia Book; http://www.urantia.org/en/urantia-book-standardized/paper-57-origin-urantia)

You are not alone

Revelation 3:20 (KJV)

(10)　Behold, I stand at the door, and knock: if any man hear　my voice, and open the door, I will come in to him, and will sup with him, and he with me.

John 3:16 KJV

See the Urantia Book; Paper 33; Administration of the LocalUniverse,page366,paragraph-2; http://www.urantia.org/urantiabookstandardized/paper33a dmi nistration-local-universe

John 10:16-18 (NKJV)

(16)　And other sheep I have which are not of this fold; them also I must bring, and they will hear My voice; and there will be one flock and one shepherd.

(17)　Therefore My Father loves Me, because I lay down My life that I may take it again.

(18)　No one takes it from Me, but I lay it down of Myself. I have power to lay it down, and I have power to take it again. This command I have received from My Father."

Matthew 26:53 (KJV)

(53)　Thinkest thou that I cannot now pray to my Father, and he shall presently give me more than twelve legions of angels?

Luke 23:34 (KJV)

(34)   Then said Jesus, Father, forgive them; for they know not what they do. And they parted his raiment, and cast lots.

Hebrews 8:5 (KJV)

(5)   Who serve unto the example and shadow of Heavenly things, as Moses was admonished of GOD when he was about to make the tabernacle: for, See, saith he, that thou make all things according to the pattern shewed to thee in the mount.

Matthew 18:14 (KJV)

(14)   Even so it is not the will of your Father which is in heaven, that one of these little ones should perish.

See the Urantia Book: Paper 38; Ministering Spirits of the Local Universe, page 422, Section-7paragraph-2; http://www.urantia.org/urantiabook-standardized/paper-38-ministering-spirits-local-universe

See the Urantia Book: Paper 38; Ministering Spirits of the Local Universe, page 424, Section-9; http://www.urantia.org/urantiabookstandardized/paper-38ministering-spirits-local-universe

See the Urantia Book: Paper 51; The Planetary Adams, page 580; http://www.urantia.org/urantiabook-standardized/paper-51planetary-adams

The Precepts and Process of Applying Faith

See Matthew 6:33(KJV)

See Romans 8:28 (KJV)

See John 14:6 (KJV)

(See John 18:36)

Luke 17:20-21 (KJV)

(20)   And when he was demanded of the Pharisees, when the kingdom of God should come, he answered them and said, The kingdom of God cometh not with observation:

(21)   Neither shall they say, Lo here! or, lo there! for, behold, the kingdom of God is within you.

See Matthew 6:33 (KJV)

See Proverbs 3:6 (KJV)

See Matthew 22:39

See Matthew 7:12

Milton Keynes UK
Ingram Content Group UK Ltd.
UKHW050725090224
437350UK00007BA/69